T0323627

Cambridge Elements ≡

Elements in Decision Theory and Philosophy
edited by
Martin Peterson
Texas A&M University

PREFERENCE CHANGE

David Strohmaier
University of Cambridge

Michael Messerli
University of Zurich

CAMBRIDGE
UNIVERSITY PRESS

Shaftesbury Road, Cambridge CB2 8EA, United Kingdom

One Liberty Plaza, 20th Floor, New York, NY 10006, USA

477 Williamstown Road, Port Melbourne, VIC 3207, Australia

314–321, 3rd Floor, Plot 3, Splendor Forum, Jasola District Centre,
New Delhi – 110025, India

103 Penang Road, #05–06/07, Visioncrest Commercial, Singapore 238467

Cambridge University Press is part of Cambridge University Press & Assessment,
a department of the University of Cambridge.

We share the University's mission to contribute to society through the pursuit of
education, learning and research at the highest international levels of excellence.

www.cambridge.org
Information on this title: www.cambridge.org/9781009475792

DOI: 10.1017/9781009181860

First published 2023

A catalogue record for this publication is available from the British Library.

ISBN 978-1-009-47579-2 Hardback
ISBN 978-1-009-18185-3 Paperback
ISSN 2517-4827 (online)
ISSN 2517-4819 (print)

Cambridge University Press & Assessment has no responsibility for the persistence or
accuracy of URLs for external or third-party internet websites referred to in this
publication and does not guarantee that any content on such websites is, or will
remain, accurate or appropriate.

Preference Change

Elements in Decision Theory and Philosophy

DOI: 10.1017/9781009181860
First published online: December 2023

David Strohmaier
University of Cambridge

Michael Messerli
University of Zurich

Author for correspondence: David Strohmaier, ds858@cam.ac.uk, Michael Messerli, mich_messerli@yahoo.de

Abstract: For most of its history, decision theory has investigated the rational choices of humans under the assumption of static preferences. Human preferences, however, change. In recent years, decision theory has increasingly acknowledged the reality of preference change throughout life. This Element provides an accessible introduction and new contributions to the debates on preference change. It is divided into three sections. In the first section, the authors discuss what preference change is and whether we can integrate it into decision theory. In the second section, they present models of preference change, including a novel proposal of their own. In the third and final section, they discuss how we can rationally choose a course of action when our preferences might change. Both the transformative experience literature and recent work on choosing for changing selves are discussed.

In recent years, decision theory has increasingly acknowledged the reality of preference change throughout life. This Element provides an accessible introduction and new contributions to the debates on preference change. This title is also available as Open Access on Cambridge Core.

This Element also has a video abstract: www.Cambridge.org/EDTP:Strohmaier

Keywords: preference change, motivation, rationality, cognition, transformation

ISBNs: 9781009475792 (HB), 9781009181853 (PB), 9781009181860 (OC)
ISSNs: 2517-4827 (online), 2517-4819 (print)

Contents

Introduction

We did not always want what we want today. A child who wanted to become a firefighter now prefers to work as a tax accountant. In fact, your authors did not always want to write a book about preference change, but at some point, they started to prefer doing so over other pastimes. Our preferences changed. Why does such change occur?

Sometimes our preferences change because we learn new things about the world; for example, one might want to write a philosophy book to fill a gap in the literature and learn that there is a distinct lack of introductions to preference change. However, not all changes in preferences lend themselves to being explained this way. Sometimes, what we want just changes fundamentally, not because we acquire information about something we already want.

This view contrasts with traditional decision theory that posits agents who possess stable preferences make rational decisions based on them. Some researchers, especially economists, have held that preferences are given and that decision theory does not consider *preference construction*. They might even assert that their decision models do not address psychological processes.[1]

We believe that decision theory should consider the psychological reality of preference change. We did not always want to work on philosophy and might lose our taste for it. Any account of us as practical agents calls for a theory of preference change to account for these personal transformations. Philosophers have many reasons to be interested in such theories of preference change, both from a descriptive and a normative perspective.

Regarding the descriptive project, philosophers might debate the reality of fundamental preference change. Are there really preferences that serve as the grounds for all other preferences? Maybe the traditional view was correct all along, and despite appearances, all that changes is our information about the world.

From a normative perspective, philosophers have proposed constraints on how our preferences *should* change. Philosophers might argue that when the reasons that motivate us change, so should our preferences. If we were no longer motivated by the reason that philosophy is an intellectual endeavour, then perhaps we should come to prefer carpentry as a career, but probably not mathematical logic.

Other philosophers debate how we can and should choose as rational agents in light of our changing preferences, addressing both a descriptive and normative question. If your preferred career might differ after a course of studies, how can you choose a course of studies as a rational agent? Which preferences should you consider?

---

[1] Warren et al. (2011) provide a description of the economic side; Lichtenstein and Slovic (2006) provide a useful overview of the psychological literature on this topic.

All these discussions centre on preference change, but they have mainly remained disconnected. This Element seeks to bring the strands together and reveal how they address being a changing agent in a complex world. In doing so, we will also draw on practical philosophers who work on topics such as rationality and autonomy. While much of this Element has a synchronic perspective (i.e. it focuses on a single point in time), notable exceptions exist (e.g. Bratman 2007).

To connect the existing philosophical work on preference change and show how it relates to our practical agency, we address three questions:

1. What is (fundamental) preference change?
2. How should we model preference change?
3. How should we choose in light of preference change?

These questions follow an intuitive progression. First, we must determine the phenomenon of interest: how does fundamental preference change fit into the basic picture of practical rationality endorsed by decision theory? Then, we ask how this phenomenon, preference change, can be modelled. What constraints are there on its dynamic? Finally, the changes in preference, which are hopefully better understood after the first two chapters raise the question of how to choose as a changing self. How can we make rational decisions based on what we prefer while being aware of the instability of our preferences? We proceed from the conceptual basis via modelling to practical conduct.

Our discussion of these questions, while not settling them conclusively, will give the reader an idea of what is at stake and how the various debates are connected. Building upon this foundation, the reader might turn themselves into an author.

1 Preferences and Preference Change

But doth not the appetite alter? A man loves the meat in his youth that he cannot endure in his age.

(Shakespeare, *Much Ado About Nothing*)

How should a rational agent choose between the options that are available to them? Decision theorists frequently answer this question using assumptions about preference relations. A rational agent chooses one option over another because they prefer it. When we are concerned with preference change, we are concerned with changes to these preference relations.

This section will introduce preference relations, their mental reality, and their role in decision theory. We will discuss what makes some preferences fundamental and argue that such fundamental preferences sometimes change. In the next section, we summarise the formal properties of the preference relation used by decision theorists to provide a foundation for our discussions.

Preference Relations

Preference relations are usually defined either in terms of a weak preference relation ($\succeq$) or in terms of a strict preference relation ($\succ$) and an indifference relation ($\sim$). These relations have intuitive interpretations in terms of wants, for example:

1. An agent weakly prefers reading a book to attending a concert if the agent wants to read *at least as much* as they want to attend the concert.
2. An agent strictly prefers hiking to watching a movie if the agent wants to hike *more* than watch a movie.
3. An agent is indifferent between hiking and reading a book if the agent wants both of them *equally*.

The three preference relations can be used to define each other using the following formulas (where '$\leftrightarrow$' stands for 'if and only if' and '$\neg$' for 'not'):

$$A \succeq B \leftrightarrow A \succ B \vee A \sim B$$

$$A \succ B \leftrightarrow A \succeq B \wedge \neg (B \succeq A)$$

$$A \sim B \leftrightarrow A \succeq B \wedge B \succeq A.$$

For example, an agent weakly prefers reading a book to attending a concert if and only if they strictly prefer reading or are indifferent between reading and a concert.

Using weak preference relations as the basic relation from which one derives the others makes some formal proofs easier. However, strict preference and indifference can be more intuitive since, in everyday language, we tend to use 'prefer' to express something similar to a strong preference relation. When Ishmael informs us that 'Queequeg, for his own private reasons, preferred his own harpoon' (Melville 1951: chapter 13), he means to convey that Queequeg wanted to use his own harpoon *rather* than having to use one provided by the whaling ship. We will use both weak and strict preference and indifference depending on the context. However, given their intuitive character, we favour strong preference and indifference.

We have specified these relations through intuitive examples, but it is commonly assumed that they must fulfil certain formal requirements that provide further specification. These might constrain the change in our preferences. We introduce a selection of these principles for illustration and use them in later discussions (for a more detailed presentation, see Hansson and Grüne-Yanoff (2017) and Bridges and Mehta (1995)).

Let A and B be any two alternatives from a set of mutually exclusive alternatives over which the strict preference and indifference relations are specified. Such a set of alternatives could, for example, be a prospective student's choice among university programmes, where only one can be selected. Then, the following requirements are considered part of the meaning of the overall preference relations (using '$\rightarrow$' for 'if' and '$\neg$' for 'not'):[2]

Asymmetry of strict preference: $A \succ B \rightarrow \neg (B \succ A)$
Symmetry of indifference: $A \sim B \rightarrow B \sim A$
Reflexivity of indifference: $A \sim A$
Incompatibility of strict preference and indifference: $A \succ B \rightarrow \neg (A \sim B)$

These requirements are rather basic and can be considered part of the semantic core of the preference conceptions. For example, it is hard to see how anyone could strictly prefer a physics course to a philosophy course and at the same time also strictly prefer the same philosophy course to the same physics course (asymmetry). Similarly, if the formal relation of indifference is supposed to be anything like our ordinary concept of indifference, an agent must be indifferent between a philosophy course and the very same philosophy course (reflexivity).[3]

In addition to these largely conceptual restrictions, preference relations are also frequently considered transitive and complete. Transitivity of strict preference and indifference requires:

Transitivity of preference: $A \succ B \wedge B \succ C \rightarrow A \succ C$
Transitivity of indifference: $A \sim B \wedge B \sim C \rightarrow A \sim C$.

Completeness demands that either strict preference or indifference holds between two options, that is,

Completeness: $(A \succ B) \vee (A \sim B) \vee (B \succ A)$.

An agent's preferences are complete for a given set of alternatives if and only if, for every two alternatives in the set, the agent either strictly prefers one alternative or is indifferent between them.

A preference relation that fulfils the sketched requirements is, in formal terms, at least a total pre-order.[4] Such a pre-order and stricter orderings would guarantee many useful properties, but transitivity and completeness have

---

[2]   The asymmetry of preference and incompatibility of preference and indifference lose plausibility if we deal with defeasible rather than overall preferences. Based on the literature, our usual assumption will be that we work with overall or all-things-considered preferences.

[3]   One can complicate the picture by introducing different descriptions of the same course. For the present purpose, we can assume that the alternatives over which the preference relation ranges have unique descriptions.

[4]   If there were no instances of indifference and only strict preference, it would be a strict total order.

been the subject of particular debate. These properties can be questioned from both a descriptive and a normative perspective (i.e. by questioning whether they describe actual human agents and whether rational agents should fulfil them).

One motivation to question completeness is straightforward: it seems unlikely that one agent could have determinate preferences for all possible comparisons. One might doubt that an agent selecting from a movie streaming service has a complete preference relation over all options. In everyday discourse, we are unlikely to blame the agent for failing to be completely opinionated.

Violations of transitivity might seem more egregious, especially from a normative perspective. If Lane prefers listening to Bowie over listening to Britney and prefers Britney over the Bee Gees, then it is at least odd not to prefer Bowie over the Bee Gees as well. However, empirical results suggest that human agents do not always conform to this principle (Tversky 1969; Fishburn 1991), and philosophers have also developed examples in which violations of transitivity appear normatively acceptable (e.g. Quinn (1990), but see also the influential money-pump arguments in favour of transitivity: Davidson et al. (1955) and Gustafsson (2010, 2013)).

For the purposes of our investigation, we are not interested in settling the status of these purported rationality restrictions but in how they relate to preference change. Three such connections are worth highlighting.

First, if completeness is not guaranteed, preference change includes cases where new preference relations are added or lost. The individual selecting from the streaming service undergoes preference change when they settle on one order over and above all the available options. Such cases are not covered by all preference change models, such as reason-based decision theory (Dietrich and List 2013a, 2013b, 2016b), which will be discussed later.

Second, the preference change model might itself be required to produce preference relations that are transitive or complete or that meet other rationality criteria. Therefore, it is often insufficient for one preference between two alternatives to change because an isolated change might violate the criteria. If Lane switches her preference between Bowie and the Bee Gees, then she also has to change her preference between Bowie and Britney or Britney and the Bee Gees to avoid a violation of transitivity.

Third, a present or threatening violation of the requirements might not only constrain preference change but also *lead* to preference change in the first place. If Logan realises that he prefers Shakespeare to Goethe and Melville to Shakespeare, this might prompt him also to prefer Melville to Goethe to avoid a violation of transitivity.

The second and third connections differ, in that only the third is concerned with the sources of preference change. The second constrains preference change without describing its source. As we will see, models of preference change differ in whether they incorporate such sources or provide more general restrictions.

A Mentalist Conception of Preferences

How does the formal description of preference relations map onto actual agents, especially human agents? When a decision theorist talks about the preferences of a human agent, which facts about the agent make their claims true or false?

Throughout this Element, we will assume that preference relations, including the indifference relation, describe mental states (i.e. 'preference' and 'indifference' denote mental states that might describe human agents). These mental states relate to two alternatives (i.e. their content is a comparison between two alternatives), and we call these mental states 'preference states'. Rory's preference for listening to Bowie over the Backstreet Boys is a preference state realised by her neural system. As such, the state has causal powers that guide her choice. In a situation where Rory has to choose between listening to Bowie and the Backstreet Boys, her preference will cause her to choose Bowie.[5]

The ontological status of preferences is controversial, and for a long time, the mentalist conception of preferences we just outlined was the minority position. Behaviourism (i.e. theories according to which preference relations merely describe behaviour) dominated the debate.[6] In particular, economists have commonly assumed, and many still do, that preferences are not realised as mental states. However, talk of preference serves as a shorthand for describing human behaviour. This behaviouristic interpretation is connected to what is known as revealed preference theory; specifically, the assumption that one alternative is strictly preferred to another if and only if the other is never chosen over the first alternative when both are available (cf. Bradley 2017: 45; Hansson and Grüne-Yanoff 2017).[7]

---

[5] We make numerous background assumptions: that Rory has correct beliefs about which songs are by Bowie, that she has the ability to select songs freely, and many more.

[6] There also exist methodological and epistemic versions of behaviourism (i.e. theories according to which our knowledge about preferences has to be inferred solely from behaviour). While we also consider these theories wrong, such a behaviourism would not rule out mentally real preferences on its own and poses fewer problems for preference change theories.

[7] This assumption was formalised as the weak axiom of revealed preferences. The axiom goes back to Samuelson's (1938) work and specifies consistency restrictions on choices based on observable quantities. There also exists a strong axiom of revealed preferences, which rules out indifference. For some critical discussion of such axioms, see Sen (1986, 1993) and Hausman (2012: chapter 3).

The behaviourist conceptions of preference survived even after behaviourism had largely been abandoned in psychology, but the general reasons for abandoning behaviourism transfer to preferences. If the talk of preferences only redescribes behaviour in other terms, then it does not explain behaviour. However, Rory might say she listens to Bowie instead of the Backstreet Boys *because* she prefers Bowie's music. At least, offering such explanations appears possible. Relatedly, if attributing preferences to agents is uniquely successful as an explanatory project, then it gives us a good reason to believe that agents indeed have preferences. If I can predict and explain Rory's music-listening behaviour by attributing various preferences to her, I appear to have captured something effective in the world.[8]

The content and exact functional role of preferences as mental states remains hotly debated. One of the most prominent options is the all-things-considered judgement interpretation of preferences, defended by Daniel Hausman (2012). Others have questioned whether such judgements are cognitively plausible (Angner 2018) or have sought to tie preferences closer to choice dispositions (e.g. Bradley 2017: 47; Guala 2019).

The exact description of preference change will clearly depend on which theory one endorses, but for our purposes, it will suffice to assume that preferences are mental entities and that, under conducive circumstances, cause choice behaviour and can be described using the type of formalisms outlined earlier, even though they might not meet all rationality criteria commonly expressed using these formalisms.

The mentalist conception of preferences will repeatedly influence our discussion of preference change. We are interested in why and how individuals change *their minds*, not just that we can express changes in behaviour as changes in preference. If formal models serve to describe humans with mental states and if the description does not sufficiently correspond to their mental states, or at least a relevant aspect of them, then the models have failed.[9]

Deciding in Light of Uncertainty

So far, we have limited our description of human choice to preferences, but that is insufficient to handle choice in the case of uncertainty (i.e. when we can only assign degrees of probability to how the world is). For this, we need fully

---

[8] For a detailed defence of a mentalist conception of preferences along these lines, see Dietrich and List (2016a), but see also Vredenburgh (2020) and Thoma (2021). For an overview of the recent debate regarding the philosophy of economics, see Vredenburgh (2021).

[9] Some deviation of the approximation is, of course, acceptable. If an agent violates transitivity in one edge case that is irrelevant to a particular situation, then a model can be forgiven for assuming transitivity.

Table 1 Basic components of Savage-type decision theory

	Disposed to Accept	*Disposed not to Accept*
Apply	Effort and Accepted	Effort and Not Accepted
Not Apply	No Effort and Not Accepted	No Effort and Not Accepted

fledged approaches to decision theory. Since the basis of preference relations can be developed in multiple ways, multiple versions of decision theory exist. Two especially influential versions are those developed by Leonard Savage (1954) and Richard Jeffrey (1990) [1965]). These versions are interchangeable for many purposes, but the treatment of preference change is not one of them. Therefore, an overview of their differences is required.

Savage-Type Decision Theory

In order to describe a decision under uncertainty, Savage-type decision theory distinguishes:

- Acts
- States of the world
- Consequences

For example, the act might be applying to a university, the relevant state of the world is whether the university is disposed to accept your application, and the consequence is whether you underwent the effort and are accepted.[10] We can express this situation in Table 1.

One might assume that you prefer expending the effort and being accepted to not expending the effort and not being accepted, which might still be better than having wasted the effort without getting accepted.[11] According to standard decision theory, whether you should apply then depends on the strength of your preferences and the probability you assign to the university being disposed to accept your application.

What we introduced here as the strength of preferences is more commonly described using a utility function. A utility function, $U(\cdot)$, takes an alternative as input and returns a real-value number as output. If one takes a mental realist perspective on utilities, they can be understood as degrees to which the

---

[10] We are referring to the dispositions of the university because we intend to deal with states of the world rather than actions by agents, which would arguably require introducing game-theoretic considerations.

[11] Or not! Maybe you prefer having at least tried and spent the effort to saving the effort. After all, that preferences can be different is a basic requirement for preference change.

alternative is wanted. We do not commit ourselves to such a perspective, but it provides an intuitive means to understand the following key formulas linking preferences:

$$A \succeq B \leftrightarrow U(A) \geq U(B).$$

Alternative A is at least as preferred as B if and only if A's utility is at least as large as B's.

$$A \succ B \leftrightarrow U(A) > U(B).$$

Alternative A is preferred to B if and only if A's utility is larger than B's.

$$A \sim B \leftrightarrow U(A) = U(B).$$

Alternative A is equally preferred as B if and only if A's utility is identical to B's.

These connecting biconditionals can still be posited from a non-realist perspective on utility, which considers it a formal tool. Formally, a utility function can be derived from preferences, provided they fulfil certain conditions, including those discussed in the previous section (see Savage 1954; Kreps 1988). In light of this derivation, one might consider the utility function as a useful shorthand for describing them.[12]

The Savage framework has two utility functions: the utility function over outcomes and the expected utility (EU) function. The fundamental utility function ranges over the consequences, such as the case where someone has applied to a university and been accepted. The EU function ranges over the acts and provides the average utility of the outcomes for this act weighted by the probability of the state of the world for that outcome.

To illustrate this concept, we have assigned arbitrary numbers in our example that allow us to calculate the EU (Table 2).

In the outlined case, the state of the world where the university is disposed to accept has a probability of 40 per cent (i.e. P(Disposed to Accept) = 0.4). The utility for spending the effort and getting accepted is 20 on our scale. Based on these numbers, we can calculate the EU for both acts:

EU(Apply) = P(Disposed to Accept) × U(Accepted & Effort) + P(Disposed to Accept) × U(Not Accepted & Effort) = 0.4 × 20 + 0.6 × −10 = 8 − 6 = 2

EU(Not Apply) = 0.4 × 0 + 0.6 × 0 = 0.

---

[12] But there might be good reasons for not doing so and asserting the psychological reality of utility functions, instead of treating them as a formal shorthand. For example, a utility function might be easier to store in the human brain. Encoding a utility function in neural associations could be more straightforward than what resulted from the evolutionary process.

Table 2 Applying the Savage-type decision theory

	P(Disposed to Accept) = 0.4	*P(Disposed not to Accept) = 0.6*
Apply	*U*(Effort & Accepted) = 20	*U*(Effort & Not Accepted) = −10
Not Apply	*U*(No Effort & Not Accepted) = 0	*U*(No Effort & Not Accepted) = 0

Assuming that EU is to be maximised, this calculation suggests that you should put in the effort and apply (2 > 0).

The EU functions, however, can be altered. Savage-type decision theory thereby distinguishes between a preference change over acts (apply vs. not apply) due to a new utility function (a change in the utility functions over outcomes) or Bayesian updating (a change in subjective probabilities).

This distinction has played a major role in debates about preference change, especially because it limits the types of preference changes that can exist. Therefore, we will return to it later.

While the framework of Savage-type decision theory is useful for many purposes, and we will draw on it accordingly, it unduly restricts the discussion of preference change.[13]

First, Savage-type decision theory precludes all discussions of preference changes over alternatives for which the framework does not assign a preference order. For example, there are no preferences over states of the world. Such a limitation does not seem psychologically required. For example, you might prefer that a university be disposed to accept you, even if the question of applying is left out of the picture. It is not obviously wrong to want the world to be a certain way, even if it being this way does not affect any choices or outcomes.

Second, preference change is limited by the dependence relations postulated by Savage's framework. Specifically, the framework requires the utility of consequences to be independent of both the state of the world in which they are realised and the action. The preferences over actions derive from the preferences over consequences (and the probabilities assigned to states) and not vice versa. However, at least at first glance, a consequence might become more appealing by virtue of the action that leads to it. For example, one might

---

[13] The discussion of these limitations in part follows Bradley (2017: chapter 1). There are also limitations we do not discuss, such as probabilistic independence between actions and states. While more general, the exclusive focus of propositions rules out, for example, preferences that have other objects, such as books, as relata. However, this is less troubling than other limitations because the relevant proposition can be that one owns or reads a book (cf. Jeffrey 1990 [1965]: 60).

get another university degree because one's preferences regarding studying over working in the industry have changed. A preference change of this sort would be ruled out by the framework, at least while one describes studying as an action.

While one can often solve such issues by re-describing the decision problem (i.e. by specifying its ontology differently), it can become unwieldy or unintuitive to do so. In such cases, the decision theory developed by Richard Jeffrey and Ethan Bolker is often more appropriate.

Jeffrey-Type Decision Theory

The Jeffrey–Bolker framework is very flexible because it takes propositions as its basic elements rather than consequences, states, and acts. Therefore, preferences in this framework describe which propositions an agent would rather see realised. For example, an agent might prefer the proposition that the university is disposed to accept an application over the proposition that the university is not disposed to accept an application. Given the generality of propositions, this leads to a more general decision-making theory.[14]

Furthermore, instead of a utility and EU function, Jeffrey-type decision theory introduces what is called a desirability function, which maps propositions to real-value numbers. The differences between the desirability and standard utility functions can be relatively subtle. In the standard interpretation of utility, a high utility indicates that the consequence is highly wanted or, in the case of EU, that the act is highly choice-worthy. Desirability, however, is often interpreted as a news-value indicator, meaning that the more the news of a certain proposition being true is wanted, the higher the proposition's desirability.[15] Therefore, the desirability for a logical truth would be zero since such a proposition being true cannot be news (for a logically omniscient agent).

Unlike the Savage-type framework, there is one desirability function and, therefore, no correspondence to the distinction between the utility and EU function (see Bradley and Stefánsson (2017: 492–493) for an interesting interpretation of desirability measures). The unified ontology of propositions also leads to this result.

Despite these differences between utility and desirability, the two types of functions can nonetheless be treated as largely equivalent for our purposes

---

[14] In fact, Bradley (2017: chapter 9) reconstructs the core of Savage's EU framework within Jeffrey's proposition-based framework.

[15] For some qualifications on the news-value conception, see Bradley (2017: 81). For a whole-hearted endorsement, see instead Ahmed (2021a).

because the formulas connecting preferences and utility also apply to the desirability function. More particularly, writing $v(\cdot)$ for the desirability function, it is the case that

$$A \succcurlyeq B \leftrightarrow v(A) \geq v(B)$$

and so on for strict preference and indifference.

Generally, we try as much as possible to adhere to the vocabulary of preferences instead of the utility or desirability function. However, since the literature on preference change also frequently uses these functions, we will use them whenever it simplifies the overall presentation.

Following these introductions, we turn to preference change, especially the difference between derived and fundamental preference change.

Derived and Fundamental Preference Change

That *some* preferences can and do change is hard to dispute. Assume we confronted you with a choice between two lottery tickets, one in the left hand and one in the right. You have to choose between these two tickets, and we will give you whichever one you choose. Presumably, you will be largely indifferent between these two options. However, if you learn that the ticket in the left hand is the winning ticket for this week's draw, your indifference will dissolve, and you will suddenly develop a clear preference in favour of it.

The process you undergo in this example is an instance of preference change, broadly construed, but this type of preference change has not greatly vexed contemporary decision theorists and philosophers. It is clear that, in this example, information drives the change in preferences. You always wanted a winning lottery ticket; you just did not know from the start that the ticket in the left hand was the winning one. What changed was the information you had, which then affected preferences derived from that information, but your *fundamental* preferences remained unchanged.

We intuitively make a difference between our fundamental preferences and preferences we derive from information (Figure 1).

This distinction between the two types of preferences and their relation to beliefs can be found in the literature under many names. Some authors prefer to distinguish intrinsic (i.e. fundamental) from extrinsic (i.e. derived) preferences (e.g. Binmore 2008: 5–6; Spohn 2009). In economics, authors distinguish between endogenous and exogenous preference change.

Both the Savage- and Jeffrey-type decision theories are well equipped to deal with derived preference change, such as in the lottery ticket example. According to Savage-type decision theory, you learn something about the states of the

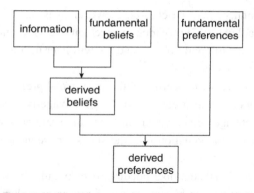

Figure 1 Fundamental vs derived preferences. Adapted
from Bradley (2009: 225).

world, namely, that the left ticket is the winning one. This piece of information
affects the EU calculation. The fundamental preferences, described by utilities
over consequences, remain untouched. All information processing is in the
standard model assumed to be captured by calculating EU.

Since Jeffrey-type decision theory does not distinguish between utility and
EU, it has another method of accounting for new information: conditioning. The
simplest and most well-known form of conditioning is classical Bayesian
conditioning, in which the agents update their degrees of belief in light of
propositions being shown to be true using their conditional degrees of belief.
That is, when one learns some proposition A, the resulting degrees of belief, Q,
follow the formula:

$$Q(\cdot) = P(\cdot|A),$$

where $P(\cdot|A)$ is the previous degrees of belief conditional on the truth of A,
which are often calculated using Bayes theorem. For example, your initial
probability of the left ticket winning might be P(left ticket winning) =
0.001 per cent. However, the conditional probability of the left ticket winning,
given that the winning number is 12345, might have been P(left ticket winning|
winning number is 12345) = 99.999 per cent since that is the number you saw on
the ticket.[16] After learning that the winning number is indeed 12345, your new
subjective probability function assigns Q(left ticket winning) = 99.999 per cent.

Such new degrees of belief then lead to changes in desirability due to their
axiomatic connections. Therefore, Bayesian conditioning captures many cases

---

[16] We are assuming that your subjective probability would not reach 1 because you might consider
perceptual failure or even hallucination to still be possible, albeit highly unlikely.

of non-fundamental preference change. However, it is not the only form of conditioning. Bradley (2017) provides an excellent overview and discussion of these different forms of conditioning, and we will later turn to one of them as a model of preference change.

In the following, we are concerned with fundamental preference change (i.e. the change of fundamental preferences). In the Savage-type decision theory, such preference change occurs when either (1) the preference ordering of the consequences or (2) the situation (i.e. the states, consequences, and/or acts) changes.

Jeffrey-type decision theory does not directly distinguish between fundamental and derived preferences because *all* preferences are taken to range over propositions. As mentioned earlier, there is also no distinction between basic and expected desirability. Nonetheless, one can introduce a distinction between more and less fundamental preferences into Jeffrey's apparatus, as shown in Bradley (2009) and outlined in Appendix A.

Our proposal, which is compatible with the Jeffrey-type decision theory, is that fundamental preferences are those that are mentally more fundamental. In fact, mentalism offers two closely intertwined ways of establishing which preferences are fundamental.

First, one can take a metaphysical perspective and argue that mental states stand in asymmetric metaphysical determination relations to each other. Your preference for the winning over the losing lottery ticket determines your preference for the lottery ticket in my left hand once you know it is the winning one. In the following, we will use the term 'grounding' for these metaphysical determination relations, but the specific grounding analysis is not decisive. For our purposes, what matters is that one state determines another in an asymmetric, non-causal manner. A preference state not grounded by any other preference states (together with beliefs) would be fundamental.

Second, one can take a normative perspective and attribute justification relations between preference states. The preference for a lottery win and the information that the lottery ticket in the left hand is the winning ticket *justifies* the preference for the left over the right ticket. In the cases we consider, the justification derives from rationality as captured by decision theory. A preference is then fundamental if and only if it is not justified by any other existing preferences (together with the relevant beliefs). When we are pressed to justify our preferences repeatedly, we reach a point where we claim to just like one alternative more than another, seemingly having reached a normatively fundamental preference.

We make the optimistic assumption that the grounding and the justification relations overlap in a well-functioning mind. This overlap partially occurs because both the grounding and the justification relation depend on the content of the involved mental states. That is, the preference for the winning lottery ticket and the belief that the left ticket is the winning ticket ground and justify the preference for the left lottery ticket by virtue of the content of these mental states.

When this overlap between justification and grounding exists, our derived preferences are grounded in preferences that justify holding them. Descriptive and normative decision theories are in agreement in this case, in that they would lead to the same model of the agent. Therefore, a mismatch can often be considered a failure of rationality.

Different types of mismatch will lead to problems of varying significance. A major problem would be if one preference partially justified another preference; for example, $A \succ B$ but grounded in its opposite (i.e. $B \succeq A$). Under normal circumstances, one should not prefer watching a movie to reading a book because one prefers reading a book over watching a movie. If such grounding were the case, one would be guaranteed to have inconsistent preferences.

Less serious, but also problematic, would be if one preference state (partially) grounded another while not justifying it (together with the relevant information). Consider the case where a preference for Bowie over Bee Gees grounds your preference for studying mathematics over sociology, despite no information providing the justificatory link between these two preferences. This outcome would be odd, to say the least, and could be considered a local breakdown of rational agency.

Whether a preference state is fundamental varies between individuals. To give an example informed by the history of philosophy, some might prefer to act according to God's commands because they prefer doing good and believe God to command the good. In contrast, others might prefer to do good because they prefer to act according to God's commands and believe God to command doing the good. In these two cases, the grounding and justification relations are reversed, but both are plausible mental constellations in which rational agents can find themselves. This example also shows that the content of mental states alone cannot explain the overlap between grounding and justification. There are also psychological facts that fix the direction of fundamentality.

The distinction between fundamental and derived preferences is further muddled by the fact that some preferences appear to be both.[17] For example, a citizen might fundamentally prefer democracy over authoritarianism while

---

[17] We would like to thank an anonymous reviewer for stressing this point.

also preferring it because they believe democracy is more effective in combating corruption. Such cases suggest two interpretive possibilities.

First, one could argue that there is one preference that is justified by other preferences and beliefs but would persist without such justification and grounding. The preference for democracy is justified by other beliefs and preferences but robust to their counterfactual absence.

Second, one might postulate two preferences that just happen to share their content. The citizen would have two preferences with the content of preferring democracy over authoritarianism.

The difference in interpretation hinges on the individuation of preference states (i.e. whether to count them based on their content or source). We believe the decision between these options to be partially a matter of psychology. With either interpretation, however, fundamental preferences exist. Therefore, such cases will not pose much of a problem in the following.

The Definition of Fundamental Preference Change

Fundamental preference change occurs if and only if at least one mentally fundamental preference state changes, including cases where a fundamental preference is added or lost. It follows that not all preference change *caused* by acquiring information is derived from preference change. Information acquisition only leads to derived preference change if it exerts its effect via the grounding or justification relations between derived beliefs and derived preference. Therefore, showing that a process causing a change in fundamental preference is also a process of information acquisition does not demonstrate that the preference change is derived. For example, an individual who was always outgoing and keen on social events might lose such preferences after receiving a traumatising letter informing them of the death of a loved one. Their preferences change because the acquired information causally affects their fundamental social preferences, not because they are grounded in even more fundamental ones that relate to the information. The letter changes who they are and does not just teach them new facts about the world.

However, derived preference change is always the result of a change in a fundamental preference or information. In the lottery ticket example, it is clear that every change is due to the new information about which is the winning ticket. If you then lost your preference for wealth over poverty, it would also explain that your derived preference for the left over the right ticket vanished.

Having laid the conceptual foundation, we turn to the question of whether such fundamental preference change exists and is not merely a conceptual possibility.

Denial of Fundamental Preferences

The existence of fundamental preference change depends on the existence of fundamental preferences. In response to Binmore's notion of intrinsic preferences, which play a similar role as fundamental preferences in our discussion, Bradley (2017: 24) suggested denying fundamental preferences. However, Binmore's intrinsic preferences also have to fulfil what he calls the Aesop principle: 'Preferences, beliefs and assessments of what is feasible should all be independent of each other' (see Bradley (2017: 23), which slightly simplifies Binmore (2008: 5)).

The exact nature of the independence – whether it is probabilistic, causal, explanatory, or any other form of independence – is not entirely clear. However, according to Bradley, Binmore asserted that '[a] preference for one thing over another is intrinsic . . . if nothing we can learn would change it' (Bradley 2017: 24).[18]

However, denying such information-resistant intrinsic preferences poses no problem in investigating and modelling fundamental preference change. As already mentioned, we expect fundamental preferences to be affected by learning new information. Consider again the case of the individual who loses their preferences for social entertainment due to receiving a traumatising letter informing them of the death of a loved one. Their original preferences cannot be intrinsic in the sense of Binmore since they were affected by information acquisition. However, they are fundamental in the sense used by us (i.e. they are mental states that are not further justified or grounded by other preference states).

One might, however, also be tempted to deny the existence of fundamental preferences as described by us. Bradley's discussion of Binmore suggests at least one reason for doing so:

> Being wealthy, attractive and in good health are no doubt all things that we might desire under a wide range of circumstances, but not in circumstances when those arouse such envy that others will seek to kill us or when they are brought about at great suffering to ourselves or others. Even rather basic preferences, such as for chocolate over strawberry ice cream, are contingent on beliefs. (Bradley 2017: 24)

This passage can be read in two ways: one that does not threaten our project and one that does. On first reading, Bradley's examples suggest that whatever preferences human agents have, they are limited to specific situations, and in other situations, agents will exhibit different preferences. However, that is entirely compatible with our project since we argue that fundamental preferences are subject to change. In some situations, an agent will have a fundamental preference

---

[18] Our discussion here neglects Binmore's (2008) endorsement of a behaviourist version of revealed preference theory.

for chocolate over strawberry ice cream, but in other situations, they will no longer do so after a preference change.

The second reading has to be that our preferences are always already conditional on other preferences and beliefs that we can ascribe to the human agents. That is, not only would human agents have different preferences when faced with other situations, it is already the case that *all* their preferences depend either on their grounding or their justification of further preferences and beliefs. We are committed to denying this and will provide one argument based on the structure of preferences and a second based on everyday discourse.

We can think of preferences as forming a network related by grounding and justifying relations. For no fundamental preferences to exist, the network must include at least one cycle or be infinite. Endorsing an infinite set of preferences conflicts with the assumed cognitive reality of preferences. Assuming that preferences are mental states, they have to be realised and stored in some form, and the human cognitive system only has a finite storage capacity.[19]

Cycles are cognitively more plausible but still controversial if the relations between preferences are those of grounding and justification, which are commonly assumed to be non-cyclical. Cycles would be much more plausible if the relevant relations between preference states were those of counterfactual dependence: if I did not have these preferences, I would not have this other one. However, grounding and justification are the defining relations in our conception, and cycles create conceptual worries for these relations.

Grounding, for example, is often made intuitive using the notion of fundamentality, but this intuitive connection would be lost if grounding allowed for cycles. How could the grounding fact be more fundamental than the grounded fact if the relationship could be reversed?[20]

The use of circular justification resembles a fallacious form of circular reasoning. In everyday discourse, it is at least odd to justify one's preference for a career in philosophy over a career in finance with a preference for thought over money and then go on to justify the latter preference upon further inquiry with a preference for a philosophical career over a career in finance. It is more natural to stop at the end instead of continuing the chain (but see Harman (1986: chapter 4) for a different view).

In addition to this argument about the structure of preferences, there is the fact that in everyday life, we often appeal to brute preferences, especially regarding tastes. Rory just prefers the fragrance of old books over that of

---

[19] One response we do not discuss here is that the brain could store a *procedure* for generating preferences.

[20] For some discussion of the relation between fundamentality and grounding, including proposals allowing for cycles, see Tahko (2018).

Chanel No. 5. We might be able to describe the causes for her preferences, pointing to formative experiences, such as the joyful reading in her childhood of a second-hand copy of Pippi Longstocking, but this falls short of deriving her preferences. No other preferences exist that justify or ground this preference for the fragrance of books (cf. Binmore 2008: 5–6), even though a *ceteris paribus* clause might constrain the situations over which they range.

We have outlined two arguments for the existence of fundamental preference, and in the following sections, we will simply assume their existence. However, not all would be lost even if we had failed to convince. Without fundamental preferences, a closely related notion remains available: desire-driven attitude change (see Bradley 2017: 209–11). Denying fundamental preferences leads to a view of attitudes as a connected network. This network can change due to changes in belief attitudes within it, changes in desire attitudes, or both. Desire-driven attitude change occurs when a change to desire attitudes leads to a change in the network. The standard decision theory models, which fail to account for fundamental preference change, also do not allow for desire-driven attitude change. Much of our presentation could be reformulated in terms of desire-driven attitude change.[21]

Explaining Preference Change Away

While most decision theorists tend to accept the existence of fundamental preferences, they have long been tempted to explain away fundamental preference change. Economists have especially tended in that direction. Avoiding fundamental preference change would make decision theory simpler and, thereby, more elegant. Economists, who tend to follow the Savage-type theory, could abide by the simple table of consequences, states, and acts and the basic preference orderings over the consequences. Such simplicity is not to be given up lightly.

One of the most influential attempts to explain away preference change can be found in the work of Stigler and Becker (1977). Their ambitious paper *De Gustibus Non Est Disputandum* (there is no disputing about tastes) suggests that there are no cases of fundamental preference change and that fundamental preferences are universal. The argumentative strategy is to suggest that 'no other approach of comparable generality and power is available' (Stigler and Becker 1977: 77) and then to deal with some of the biggest challenges to the assumption of stable and universal preferences, including addiction and fashion.

Discussing the case of heroin addiction, Stigler and Becker (1977: 80) propose that there exists an underlying commodity called 'euphoria' that can be produced with input from heroin. To model addiction, one can then assume that

---

[21] Much of it but not all. Problems would arise for the sources-of-change models discussed in the second half of Chapter 2. We will not discuss this difficulty further.

1. the consumption of euphoria reduces what, in economic terms, would be the future stock of euphoria capital, raising the costs of producing euphoria in the future;
2. the demand for euphoria is sufficiently inelastic that heroin use would increase over time.

With these assumptions, an economic model of addiction behaviour can be created without postulating fundamental preference change.

Fashions are another candidate for preference change that might bother economists. Individuals who preferred a suit jacket with shoulder pads in the 80s no longer do so, even though it is hard to see what new relevant information they would have acquired at first glance. The visual experience was presumably the same back then as it is now. So, one might think what has changed is the basic taste for certain visual experiences over others, perhaps simply because we have become accustomed to them. However, Stigler and Becker again suggest that the behaviour towards fashion is best explained by a preference for an underlying commodity; in this case, style as a form of social distinction. In order to achieve this form of distinction, fashion items must be new and 'the newness must be of a special sort that requires a subtle prediction of what will be approved novelty' (Stigler and Becker 1977: 88). Therefore, fashion will be subject to change, and being fashionable (i.e. achieving social distinction via fashion) requires skill and effort.

With these and other examples, Stigler and Becker show how fundamental preference change can be explained away, in that a stable-preference model of the phenomenon can be found. However, showing that such stable-preference models are available is not quite the same as accepting that they *should* be used to explain away preference change. As usual, many models with inconsistent interpretations will fit the same data; so we must consider their plausibility and various epistemic virtues. Therefore, to challenge Stigler and Becker's approach, one can either point to cases where the interpretation of a model with preference change has plausibility due to known causal paths or to cases where a model with preference change enjoys other epistemic virtues to at least the same degree as a preference-stable model.

To illustrate how a preference change model might be more plausible due to known causal pathways, consider Stigler and Becker's heroin example again. We know that drugs such as heroin interfere with the normal functioning of the human neural system. Given the assumption that preferences are mental states realised by the neural system, there is a clear causal pathway of how heroin might affect fundamental preferences. A substrate that grounds preferences is affected by its consumption, sometimes to such an extent that it would be surprising if no fundamental preferences were affected. So, at least for those accepting the mentalist conception of preferences, there are good reasons to believe that fundamental preference change occurs in cases involving marked changes to the neural system.

Heroin consumption is not the only event where we have good reasons to believe that there is an effect on the neural substrate of preferences. Many of these events, such as sleep deprivation and brain damage, may appear deviant (i.e. as an aberration from proper functioning). However, humans also undergo events during a healthy life that might affect their fundamental preferences. For example, one might expect the physical maturation of children and pregnancy to causally affect the realisers of preferences. Any stable-preference model that deals with such instances would also have to provide arguments as to why the common assumption of causal effects is wrong, something Stigler and Becker do not provide.[22]

Having discussed how known causal pathways might support preference change models, we now consider other epistemic virtues that might support preference change. As quoted towards the beginning of this section, Stigler and Becker (1977: 77) have suggested that 'no other approach [than that of stable and universal tastes] of comparable generality and power is available'. However, taken at face value, this claim is wrong. Generality and power on their own do not appear to favour a model with stable preferences over a model with changeable preferences. After all, models with changing preferences are (typically) a generalisation of models with stable preferences. To be charitable, one should not take the claim of Stigler and Becker at face value. Instead, their point must be that models with stable preferences have *sufficient* generality and power to explain all phenomena while being simpler and avoiding ad hoc attributions of preference change.

It is undoubtedly true that adding preference change can complicate models, but sometimes the efforts to avoid preference change also lead to considerable complications. In the case of both addiction and fashion, Stigler and Becker had to introduce some underlying object of interest – euphoria or social distinction – in addition to further assumptions, such as an inelastic demand for euphoria. At least in some cases, the required assumptions will be so complex that a model attributing preference change is simpler. To quote Bradley's response to Stigler and Becker: 'The sorts of suppositions that will need to be made about changes to underlying beliefs in order to preserve the invariance of tastes may well be as ad hoc as the assumptions about taste changes that they are supposed to replace and may be no more constrained by the empirical evidence' (Bradley 2009: 239).

---

[22] However, we also have to admit that such instances of preference change might also be less well-captured by the models of preference change discussed in Chapter 2. There remains a gap in the philosophical literature, but see Grüne-Yanoff and Hansson (2009: 176–77).

The accusation of making ad hoc assumptions cuts both ways, and sometimes the assumptions required for vindicating stable tastes might be even more ad hoc than that of changing preferences. Therefore, the reference to epistemic virtues alone does not vindicate stable-preference models.

This argument against the position taken by Stigler and Becker can be generalised to work against a strategy for avoiding attributing fundamental preference change (described and criticised by Dietrich and List (2013b: 627–28)). This strategy has two steps:

1. The first introduces a sufficiently fine ontology of alternatives over which fixed preferences are taken to range.
2. The second then explains away any apparent examples of fundamental preference change as the result of information acquisition.

Consistent with this general strategy, Stigler and Becker can also be understood as fine-graining alternatives. For example, they fine-grain the choice between fashion items by introducing social distinction to the goods that matter and then explain away preference change as a change in information about social distinction. What has changed is not a fundamental preference relation that ranges over alternatives such as suits with and without extravagant shoulder pads, but the information about which of those suits contribute to (positive) social distinction.

A general problem with this strategy becomes apparent at this higher level of abstraction. Any preference change would have to satisfy the constraints of Bayesian information learning, including dynamical consistency (see Dietrich and List 2013b: 628). While one might be able to meet those constraints by fine-graining alternatives and making more assumptions about the agent's situation, the resulting model might very well be less appealing than one that includes preference change. Therefore, Dietrich and List end their discussion of this strategy with a similar conclusion to Bradley:

> Interpretationally, the main cost of remodelling every preference change in informational terms would be a significant expansion of the ontology over which the agent would have to hold beliefs and preferences. This is a cognitively demanding model of an agent, which does not seem to be psychologically plausible. We would preserve rational choice theory's parsimony with respect to the assumption of fixed preferences only at the expense of sacrificing parsimony with respect to the cognitive complexity ascribed to the agent. (Dietrich and List 2013b: 628)

Explaining away fundamental preference change in all cases is a strategy unlikely to succeed. Its epistemic virtues of a stable-preference theory do not cover its costs. Nonetheless, those convinced by the reality of fundamental preference change, including your humble authors, are well-advised to consider explanatory strategies such as those of Stigler and Becker. It can be all too easy to postulate preference change to explain whatever puzzle is at hand, especially without any rigorous preference change models. Someone convinced by the ubiquity of fundamental preference change might have failed to consider the role of social distinction in fashion, as described by Stigler and Becker. Identifying the exact limits of these different types of models is a philosophically interesting challenge. They might all share the same predictions of the behavioural data but differ profoundly in their description of human agency.

Furthermore, in 1977, Stigler and Becker could have justifiably claimed that no models incorporating preference change had reached the level of sophistication and rigour achieved by stable-preference models. As we will see, the situation has improved since then, even though models of fundamental preference change remain underdeveloped. However, the solution is not to avoid preference change attribution and add increasingly dubious assumptions to stable-preference models but to develop models of preference change. Philosophical work remains to be done in laying the conceptual and theoretical foundations for such models. We turn to this project in the next chapter.

2 Models of Preference Change

Two Input-Assimilation Models of Preference Change

So far, we have introduced the nature of preferences and decision theory and defended the existence of fundamental preference change. We now turn to specific models of preference change.

Conceptually, we can distinguish between normative and descriptive models of preference change. While normative models prescribe how individuals' preferences should change over time, descriptive models describe how preferences do change over time (without assuming that they should change optimally).[23] However, many models of preference change involve both descriptive and normative aspects and are, in fact, mixed models.

To illustrate, consider one of the earliest formal models of preference change proposed by Cohen and Axelrod (1984). They outlined a dynamic model in which an agent adopts a policy for action, observes the results of this policy, which leads them to update their beliefs and preferences, and then implements a policy that has been changed accordingly. Overlooking its further details, it is striking how their model combines descriptive and normative aspects. While it

---

[23] We thank an anonymous reviewer for bringing this to our attention.

makes the descriptive proposal that *surprise* causes preference change,[24] it is normative because a preference-changing agent performs better in maximising an output than a static agent, at least for an extensive range of parameters. Given that arguments in decision theory often take the form that achieving more is better than less (if you are so smart, why aren't you rich?), Cohen and Axelrod's (1984) approach also makes a normative case for their specific version of preference change.

In this chapter, we will see that more recent models of preference change, including our own proposal, also incorporate both normative and descriptive assumptions. We start with two comparable approaches, one based on preference logic and one based on Jeffrey-type Bayesian decision theory. Both types of approach produce 'input-assimilation' models and answer the following question (Hansson 1995: 2, 2001: 43):[25] given that one or more preferences have locally changed (input), how can the overall preference ordering of the agent be updated (assimilated)? Such models are normative, in that they prescribe that an agent should strive to maintain consistency in his preferences over time and that they rule out certain types of preference changes as irrational. However, descriptive considerations will also become apparent.

Preference-Logic Models of Preference Change

Multiple preference logic-based approaches to preference change exist, but we focus on an AGM-based model.[26] The AGM model was originally a model of belief change and is named after three eminent researchers (Alchourrón et al. 1985). Only later have its ideas been used to model preference change.

Hansson and Grüne-Yanoff have offered some of the most prominent applications of the AGM model to preference change (Hansson 1995; Grüne-Yanoff and Hansson 2009; Grüne-Yanoff 2013).[27] The bases for these applications are the formal preference relations discussed in chapter 1, which are then incorporated in propositional logic without addressing uncertainty, as the Savage- and Jeffrey-type decision theories do.

---

[24] Cohen and Axelrod (1984: 31) defined surprise as 'the difference between the utility experienced as the result of an action and the utility expected to result from that action'. Such utility misprediction has been extensively discussed in the psychological literature (see Rachman and Arntz (1991); Wilson et al. (2000); and Levine et al. (2012)).

[25] Both types of model can also be described as 'perturbation-propagation' (Bradley 2017: 245) or 'consistency-preservation' (Grüne-Yanoff 2013: 2624) models.

[26] In addition to the AGM-inspired models using propositional logic, modal logics of preference change have been widely discussed (see Girard (2008); van Benthem and Liu (2007); van Benthem (2009); de Jongh and Liu (2009); and Liu (2010)).

[27] For other models of preference change that are nonetheless inspired by the AGM belief change model (see Alechina et al. (2013) and Cadilhac et al. (2015)).

We start with a set of alternatives, A, which might, for example, be a set of book genres over which an agent has preferences:

$A = \{\text{SciFi, Fantasy, Crime}\}.$

In this context, we can represent a preference relation R as a set of tuples, each comprising two alternatives that are compared. For example, if Lane prefers science fiction (SciFi) to crime and fantasy literature and also prefers crime to fantasy literature, then her preference ranking can be represented as follows:

$R_{\text{Lane}} = \{\langle\text{SciFi, Fantasy}\rangle, \langle\text{SciFi, Crime}\rangle, \langle\text{Crime, Fantasy}\rangle,$

$\langle\text{SciFi, SciFi}\rangle, \langle\text{Crime, Crime}\rangle, \langle\text{Fantasy, Fantasy}\rangle\}.$

Each tuple ranks the first option at least as highly as the second. In this example, Lane is shown to have a reflexive and transitive weak preference relation.

Such a preference relation R then renders valid a set of preference sentences $[R]$ similar to the semantics of propositional logic (see again Hansson 1995: 8; Grüne-Yanoff 2013: 2626). For example, the tuple $\langle\text{SciFi, Fantasy}\rangle$ validates the proposition that Lane weakly prefers SciFi to Fantasy (i.e. the preference sentence 'SciFi $\succcurlyeq$ Fantasy'). Expressed formally:

$\langle A, B\rangle \in R \leftrightarrow A \succcurlyeq B \in [R].$

The absence of a preference sentence, represented by the variable α, from the set of sentences validates its negation:

$\alpha \notin [R] \leftrightarrow \neg\alpha \in [R].$

Hansson and Grüne-Yanoff also used the connectives of propositional logic (i.e. conjunction, disjunction, and the material conditional). The formal description of conjunction would be:

$\alpha \in [R] \wedge \beta \in [R] \leftrightarrow \alpha \wedge \beta \in [R].$

In essence, the basic preference sentences express a simple (weak) preference for one alternative over another and further sentences are constructed using negation and standard logical connectives.

Representing a preference relation as a set of tuples and the associated sentences allows for incomplete, intransitive, and further unusual preferences. However, despite this flexibility, Hansson and Grüne-Yanoff consider such a set of tuples insufficient to represent certain plausible states of mind. Specifically, agents might be in a state where they hold one or another preference but have not settled on one yet.

Consider a case in which the agent knows that they prefer either *The Dispossessed* (D) or *The Lord of the Rings* (LotR) to *Death on the Nile* (DotN) but cannot remember which one it was. Here, the preference sentence $D \succ DotN \lor LotR \succ DotN$ holds, but neither $D \succ DotN$ nor $LotR \succ DotN$ holds.[28] Regarding the present formalism, the disjunction of two preference sentences might be valid without either being valid. To solve this problem, Hansson introduced a set **R** of preference relations and defined that a preference sentence holds for **R** if and only if all R in **R** validated it. In the case of the three books, **R** might be a set of two preference relations, R_1 and R_2, where the first validates the first disjunct ($D \succ DotN$) and the second validates the second ($LotR \succ DotN$).

The formal apparatus allowed Hansson (1995: 10, 2001: chapter 4) to describe four elementary types of preference change:

1. Revision: a new preference sentence (e.g. $A \succcurlyeq B$) is included in the preference model **R**.
2. Contraction: a preference sentence is lost from the preference model **R**.
3. Addition: a new alternative becomes available for the preference model **R**.
4. Subtraction: an alternative for the preference model **R** is lost.

Hansson provides a complete description of these types, but we will limit ourselves to a largely informal discussion of how to make the four types of preference change specific. After all, there are many ways to include a sentence in a preference model.

To visualise the problem, consider a case where an agent neither weakly prefers the movie *Totoro* to *Bambi* nor vice versa. Assume that their **R** includes only the preference relations R_1 and R_2, where the first one validates only *Totoro* $\succcurlyeq$ *Bambi* and the second only *Bambi* $\succcurlyeq$ *Totoro*, but neither validates both. If the agent undergoes a revision that *Totoro* $\succcurlyeq$ *Bambi* is validated for them, then the second relation (R_2) has to be different. However, it could be changed so that:

- *Totoro* $\succcurlyeq$ *Bambi* is only added to what R_2 makes true, in which case the R_2 would specify indifference between the two movies.
- Or the earlier *Bambi* $\succcurlyeq$ *Totoro* in R_2 would be lost, in which case the agent represented by **R** now strictly prefers Totoro.

---

[28] One might respond that in this case, the agent only lacks knowledge of their preferences but still has determinate preferences. But from a psychological realist perspective, this is not obviously the case. It could be that the agent is completely unable to recall what the content of the two books was and only recalls the two titles because they wrote them down. Under these assumptions, they seem to lack the relevant knowledge to form the mentally real preference states that would resolve the disjunction.

The description given so far does not settle which version is correct.

To make the four types of preference change specific, Hansson suggests that the preference model before the change should be maximally similar to that of the model afterwards. Put differently: the change should be conservative. This move requires a notion of distance. Many such notions can be defined simply by counting how many preference sentences were true for the first model but not the second and vice versa and then adding those two counts together. The maximally similar model is the one for which the added count is the smallest.

However, Hansson (1995: 12) suggests a slightly more complex distance metric, where some preferences change before others. Specifically, he proposes that the revision operation includes a so-called priority index that specifies alternatives that are 'loosened' during the revision. When multiple ways to undergo preference change are open, the change that concerns the loosened alternatives should occur with priority. For example, when Lane re-reads *The Lord of the Rings* and concludes that it is better than *Dune*, her experience might loosen her preferences for SciFi and Fantasy books but not travel guides. On Hansson's account, that means that if a change in Lane's preferences over genre novels can help avoid a preference change over travel guides, then the first change will occur. Her preferences over genre novels have been loosened and so should have priority in change.

The general conservative constraints imposed by Hansson and Grüne-Yanoff can be motivated in at least three ways (see Grüne-Yanoff 2013: 2629). First, the change process might have cognitive costs. Presumably, the agent seeks to ensure that the resulting new preferences are consistent and fulfil various prior commitments. The smaller the preferences change, the fewer the ways of newly violating these restrictions.

Second, the existing preferences might have been reached through an investment, either cognitively or otherwise, and therefore can be seen as a form of 'accumulated capital' (Grüne-Yanoff 2013: 2629). Regarding biographies, Rory might prefer *The Power Broker* to *The Life of Johnson* because she spent months reading both volumes and evaluating their multifaceted qualities. Given the effort it takes to establish such well-considered preferences on the matter, they should not be discarded without need.

Third, the functioning of preferences in human conduct might require stability. Grüne-Yanoff highlights the role of preferences in personal identity and long-time planning. Some social coordination functions might also be better served by stability than fluctuations not forced by the preference change-inducing event.

All three considerations are most easily understood and supported if preferences are assumed to be cognitively real. If preferences were merely used to describe behaviour, there would be no cognitive cost, and it would be challenging to see how they would accumulate cognitive capital or play a direct function in cognitive life. Recovering these three reasons from a behaviourist perspective would require considerable conceptual work. Therefore, the arguments by Hansson and Grüne-Yanoff illustrate the deep intertwinement between the ontology of preferences and theories of preference change. This intertwinement is also between descriptive and normative modelling. The cognitive roles ascribed by these arguments are a matter of descriptive inquiry and modelling, but they are used to impose normative constraints.

As the name suggests, preference logic deals with preferences, but decision theorists prefer to work with utility or desirability functions. We now discuss how Bayesian decision theorists can deal with fundamental preference change.

Bayesian Models of Preference Change

The flexibility of the Bayesian framework makes it comparatively easy to introduce fundamental preference change into Jeffrey-type decision theory. While the conditioning approach was initially intended to deal with new evidence, there is no reason to limit it in such a way. Bradley's (2017) work on conditioning explicitly covers changes in preferences, including what he describes as desire-driven changes. Given the variety of ways of conditioning, not all of them can be covered; instead, we focus here on what Bradley calls 'generalised conditioning'.

Let P and V stand for the old degrees of belief and desirability and Q and W for the new degrees of belief and desirability (i.e. the degrees after the change has occurred). Furthermore, we need the notion of a partition of the alternatives, which are in the Jeffrey-framework propositions. A partition of a set of propositions is a set of subsets that do not share any elements but together include all elements in the original set of propositions. So, if the propositions are:

- tomorrow I read *The Power Broker*,
- tomorrow I will work on preference change, or
- tomorrow is a Sunday,

then one partition would be the set: {{Tomorrow I read *The Power Broker*, Tomorrow is Sunday}, {Tomorrow I will work on preference change}}. For brevity, we write the partition $\mathbf{A} = \{\alpha_i\}$, where α_1, α_2, and so on are the various members of the partition, which are themselves sets of propositions.

Given this notation, the new pair of degrees can be obtained from the old by generalised conditioning if and only if for all propositions β and for all α_i in $\mathbf{A}$ (such that $P(\beta|\alpha_i) > 0$), the following equations hold (2017: 202):

$$Q(\beta) = \sum_i P(\beta|\alpha_i) \cdot Q(\alpha_i).$$

This first equation describes the new degrees of beliefs. They result from multiplying the previous conditional probabilities for the proposition β with the new probabilities for the partition elements across the partition. More important for our purposes is the second equation describing the new degrees of desirability:

$$W(\beta) = \sum_i [V(\beta|\alpha_i) + W(\alpha_i)] \cdot Q(\alpha_i|\beta).$$

Given the connection between desirability and preferences (i.e. an alternative is weakly preferred to another if and only if it has at least as high a desirability), the second equation describes a type of preference change. These equations might appear opaque, and we cannot provide here all of the well-developed justification in Bradley's (2017) book and (2007) paper. However, to hint at some of the intuition regarding the desirability equation, note that $V(\beta|\alpha_i) + W(\alpha_i) = W(\beta\alpha_i)$. That is, deriving the new desirability for β involves taking the new joint desirability for β with each proposition from the partition and then weighing this joint desirability by the new conditional probability of the relevant proposition from the partition given β. Roughly, we consider the new desirability of all ways in which β could be true and weigh them by the relevant probability.

Generalised conditioning covers cases where preferences over a given set of alternatives change direction. Not covered are cases where:

1. an agent acquires or loses a preference between two alternatives;
2. an agent becomes aware or loses awareness of an alternative.

In his effort to make Bayesian decision theory more realistic, Bradley has provided a way of dealing with these cases. The core idea will be broadly familiar since it also takes inspiration from the AGM model of belief change (see Bradley 2017: 245). As we did in our discussion of Hansson and Grüne-Yanoff, we will provide a broad outline without all the formal details.

To address the loss and gain of preferences, Bradley introduces the notion of avatars. The main intuition is that an agent can be thought of as a group of agents, called avatars, that disagree amongst themselves. If Rory has not yet settled on the desirability of various courses she might pick this term, she can be modelled as having multiple avatars that differ regarding the desirability of these courses while sharing attitudes regarding other alternatives on which Rory has a settled state of mind.[29] For example, $Rory_1$, her first avatar, might assign $V(\text{biology}) = 10$ and $V(\text{sociology}) = 5$, while $Rory_2$ might assign the numbers in reverse (i.e. $V(\text{biology}) = 5$ and $V(\text{sociology}) = 10$). If Rory the person settles on the first desirabilities, this can be modelled as her losing the second avatar that was previously in contradiction with this assignment.

The avatar approach greatly resembles the preference-logic approach of having a preference model **R** that is a set of multiple preference relations R_1, $R_2, \ldots, R_n$. In both cases, the represented agent is said to prefer one alternative over another if and only if all components (i.e. all avatars or all preference relations) validate such a preference. Nonetheless, there are considerable differences. First, Bradley's avatars are taken to have desirability and probability functions, which impose stricter criteria on the avatars than the existence of a preference model **R** requires. Second, Bradley's approach does not include the notion of preference sentences, which could then be extended using logical connectives.[30]

These differences could be addressed by extending and adapting Hansson's preference logic and Bradley's Bayesian approach. One could require the preference model **R** to be such that the relations it includes allow the construction of desirability functions, and one might define a language of preference sentences for Bradley's framework. However, there are reasons not to do so. The two approaches have different purposes. The preference-logic approach is better suited to cases where the modeller wants to make minimal assumptions. Bradley's extension is appropriate in cases where the full power of Bayesian decision theory is required.

Having covered losing or acquiring a preference state, the option of becoming aware or losing awareness of an alternative remains. To model such changes in awareness, Bradley distinguishes the modeller's domain from the agent's. Simply put, there is a truly available set of alternatives and a subset of which the agent is aware. From the perspective of Bradley's project, the question is which restrictions rationality imposes on extending and restricting the agent's domain of awareness. Bradley (2017: 255–60) primarily endorses conservative criteria that describe the preservation of attitudes. In the case of domain extension, the

---

[29] We do not describe these avatars and their subjective probability and desirability functions as actually being realised as mental entities. While the notion of avatars is highly useful for modelling purposes, it is very questionable to attribute any cognitive reality to them, especially when their subjective probability and desirability functions range over a large number of alternatives. Having not only one but multiple such functions realised would be an extreme cognitive burden.

[30] The propositions that serve as the range for the desirability and probability functions can include logical connectives, but this level is to be distinguished from that of preference (or desirability) sentences.

agent's new probabilities and desirabilities should be the same as the original unconditional probabilities and desirabilities. In the case of domain restriction, the new probabilities and desirabilities should be the same as the old probabilities and desirabilities conditioned on what is to become the new smaller domain of alternatives. Put differently, when extending one's domain, the previous attitudes are preserved as attitudes conditioned on the previous domain. In contrast, when restricting one's domain, the previous attitudes conditioned on the sub-domain are preserved as unconditional attitudes.

We have already encountered conservative requirements in discussing Hansson's and Grüne-Yanoff's approaches. However, as with the case of avatars and preference models, there are significant differences. Grüne-Yanoff (2013) has criticised in detail that Bradley's approach does not include a similarity measure between desirability functions, which would govern the change of such desirabilities. It is not the case in Bradley's approach that an agent will necessarily develop the most similar desirability function, given the required changes and constraints of rationality. The rigidity that Bradley formalised using conditional attitudes does not have the same restrictive force. While similarity measures could also be introduced into Bradley's approach, doing so is not without challenges (see Grüne-Yanoff (2013) for details).

Beyond Input-Assimilation Models: Sources of Change

In this section, we move beyond input-assimilation models of preference change and consider how to model the sources of change. Such models need to specify constraints on how preferences change and the conditions for *whether* preferences change. To distinguish them from input-assimilation models, we call them sources-of-change models.

The reader might wonder whether sources-of-change models fall into the domain of philosophy. In particular, one might believe that rationality imposes negligible constraints on the sources of preference change. Making this assumption, one might hold that models of these sources are purely psychological, not normative and of no philosophical interest. Unsurprisingly, we disagree with this view, and we do so for at least two reasons:

1. Philosophers are not just investigating normative questions but are also invested in descriptive endeavours. For example, philosophers of the social sciences pursue questions about the descriptive adequacy of agency models, including sources-of-change models. Considering the conceptual space of such models is a worthy endeavour for philosophers.

2. Sources of preference change and their impact fall into the domain of practical rationality. One way to see this is to consider our normative

attitudes towards such change. For example, preference change is often considered unreasonable due to its source: one should not change one's preference for one's life partner due to the current weather. Being a good-weather partner is improper. Indeed, it might not only be morally reprehensible, but if such unconnected patterns proliferate, one might question whether the system is still a rational agent. Sources-of-change models might allow for describing such constraints or criticise systems for failing to do so.

In the following, we introduce reason-based decision theory and the commitment-based theory of preference change as two sources-of-change models.

Reason-Based Decision Theory

When Ishmael told us that 'Queequeg, for his own private reasons, preferred his own harpoon', he implied that our preferences could be grounded in reasons. Developed by Dietrich and List (2013a, 2013b, 2016b), reason-based decision theory captures how shifts in such motivating reasons induce preference change.

You might be motivated by the appeal of being famous and therefore prefer a career as a social media influencer to that of a decision theorist one day, while the next day, being famous does not serve as a motivating reason to you anymore, and your preference reverses. You stopped considering that reason, and, as a result, your preferences are no longer the same.[31]

In order to model such preference changes, reason-based decision theory postulates:

1. an underlying set of motivationally salient properties;
2. a weighing relation over the power set of properties.

Together, they ground the fundamental preferences of each agent.

Let us start with a set, called P, of potentially motivating properties for a university course:

P = {includes lots of mathematics (LM), taught by a great professor (GP), ...}.

Only some of these properties will be motivationally salient for each human agent who has to choose between courses. Dietrich and List call the set of motivationally salient properties the agent's motivational state. We can think of

---

[31] By somewhat simplifying and combining the formulations of the cited papers by Dietrich and List, we treat potentially motivationally salient properties as reasons.

the motivational state as specifying the agent's motivating reasons. Formally, the agent's motivational state, M, is a subset of the set of all properties, P (i.e. $M \subseteq P$).

Many combinations of properties can be motivating (i.e. many Ms that form a set of all potential motivational states). Let **M** denote this set of all motivational states that are psychologically possible. In our case, **M** would be as follows:

$$\mathbf{M} = \{\{LM, GP\}, \{GP\}, \{LM\}, \{\} \ldots\}.$$

For example, Paris might be motivated to choose a university programme because it is taught by a great professor (GP) and/or includes lots of mathematics (LM); then, we can write for Paris that $M = \{LM, GP\}$.

Furthermore, Dietrich and List introduce a binary relation $\geq$, called the weighing relation, over **M**. For example, the weighing relation might put the singleton set of being taught by a GP over the empty set. If and only if the (weak) weighing relation ranks one set of properties over another, the higher-ranked set is at least as choice-worthy as the other.

A complete weighing relation allows for deducing the agent's preferences over alternatives for each possible motivational state in **M** as follows: for each alternative, one identifies the set of *motivationally salient* properties it instantiates and then finds the place of this set in the weighing relation. That place specifies the rank of the alternative.[32]

We will illustrate this with the case of Paris choosing between university programmes which can be described as combinations of two properties: being taught by a GP and including LM. The options are:[33]

- Medicine is taught by a GP but does not include LM (GP, not LM).
- Physics includes LM but is not taught by a GP (LM, not GP).
- Biology has neither of the two properties (not LM, not GP).

As already mentioned, Dietrich and List further postulate an underlying ordering of the possible motivational states given by the agent's weighing relation. In Paris' case, this ordering might look like this:[34]

$$\{LM, GP\} > \{GP\} > \{LM\} > \{\}.$$

The set of all properties is ranked above the sets containing one property and the empty set. This ordering induces a preference ordering for the three

---

[32] For a formally more rigorous description that links this procedure to choice, see Dietrich and List (2016b: 189).

[33] Our example follows Dietrich and List (2013b: 619–20).

[34] The ordering would not have to be strict. We only use strict ordering for illustration.

programmes, given a motivational state in which Paris could find herself (Table 3). Assuming both properties are salient, Paris strictly prefers Medicine to Physics and Physics to Biology. By contrast, if Paris is not motivated by any of the two reasons that could guide her choice, then she will simply be indifferent between all available options. If no properties are motivationally salient, then no alternative can instantiate a motivationally salient property.

Dietrich and List's framework combines reasons, as commonly discussed in philosophical investigations of practical rationality, with decision theory. The framework clearly draws upon the philosophical literature and has both normative and description ambitions.

Given the framework's versatility, it is unsurprising that Dietrich and List have developed it in multiple directions. One of them was to propose it as an answer to the question of where preferences come from (see the title of Dietrich and List (2013b)). A comprehensive answer to this question requires a theory of preference change, and we will evaluate reason-based decisions only regarding this requirement. Specifically, we will address two issues:

- Can it cover all cases of preference change?
- Is the reason-based framework a theory of *fundamental* preference change?

The Scope of Reason-Based Decision Theory

Dietrich and List (2016b: 200–06) have sketched various applications of reason-based decision theory, the explanation of framing effects, reference-dependent choices, and more. However, it is quite plausible that reason-based decision theory cannot be the one theory of all preference changes. In particular, Dietrich and List's assumption of a stable weighing relation over sets of properties limits the theory's scope.

Assume that Paris' weighing relation takes the following form:

$$\{GP\} > \{\} > \{LM, GP\} > \{LM\}.$$

This weighing relation always orders sets of properties that include LM as lower than the empty set. Consequently, no matter which properties are motivationally salient, Paris can never strictly prefer a course that requires LM to one taught by a GP (i.e. in our example, she can never strictly prefer physics to medicine).[35] To model a transformation of Paris into an ardent student of mathematics would

---

[35] We are, for the sake of illustration, still assuming that there are no other properties that could be salient.

Table 3 Reason-based decision theory

$M =$	{LM, GP}	{GP}	{LM}	{}
Preferences over property sets	{LM, GP} ≻ {GP} ≻ {LM} ≻ {}	{LM, GP} ~ {GP} ≻ {LM} ≻ {}	{LM, GP} ~ {LM} ≻ {GP} ≻ {}	{LM, GP} ~ {LM} ~ {GP} ~ {}
Preferences over programmes	Medicine ≻ Physics ≻ Biology	Medicine ≻ Physics ~ Biology	Physics ≻ Medicine ~ Biology	Physics ~ Medicine ~ Biology

require a change in the weighing relation. However, Dietrich and List do not describe how such changes might occur and treat the relation as stable.

It is, of course, an option to double down and assert that if Paris had such a weighing relation, it could never change, and, given the assumptions of our example, Paris could never strictly prefer physics to medicine. However, this does not appear to us a constraint of practical rationality. It is hard to see what principle of rationality would force us always to weigh sets of reasons the same way.

If it is not a normative or conceptual constraint, such a change would presumably be nomologically impossible due to the laws of psychology. However, postulating such a psychological law appears rather bold to us, especially since such restrictive laws are generally hard to come by in psychology. It is more likely that reason-based decision theory only accounts for a specific type of preference change (i.e. change due to differences in the motivational salience of reasons) and that other types of change must also be postulated.

Is the Change Fundamental?

As discussed in Chapter 1, we are interested in fundamental preference change, but one might question whether the preferences that change in reason-based decision theory are fundamental. As we have proposed, a preference state is fundamental if it is not grounded or justified by other preference states and beliefs. However, in the case of reason-based decision theory, it might seem that the preferences over alternatives are grounded and justified by another preference-like relation (i.e. the weighing relation over sets of properties). The main difference is that preferences are derived from a fundamental weighing relation and motivational states instead of beliefs.

Regarding whether the weighing relation is a preference relation, we believe that it should be considered as such for the purposes of asking the question of fundamentality. This interpretation aligns with the intent of the framework's proponents. In an early paper, Dietrich and List (2013b: 628–30) left open whether the weighing relation should be considered a preference relation, but they later (2016b) came to be at peace with that description and used it themselves. Formally, the weighing relation strongly resembles a preference relation.

To render the relations different, one could propose a rationality requirement for one while denying it for the other.[36] For example, one could claim that the

---

[36] In imposing such different criteria, one has to be careful to make the preference ordering still derivable from the weighing relation. How would one derive cyclical preferences from an acyclical weighing relation?

weighing relation has to be a strict ordering without indifference, while a preference ordering could include indifference. However, it seems to us that such a distinction would be primarily technical. Since we do not see the basis for this distinction in practical rationality, it does not really touch upon the substance of whether preferences over alternatives were similarly derived as preferences over actions in the case of uncertainty. Therefore, the reason-based decision theory does not account for truly *fundamental* preference change after all.

The Role of Commitment in Preference Change

As a capstone for our discussion of sources-of-change models, we want to connect them to the input-assimilation model of Hansson and Grüne-Yanoff, which distinguishes two tiers of alternatives during revision. Some preferences were loosened and were, therefore, less robust during the change.[37]

Since Hansson and Grüne-Yanoff were working within the framework of input-assimilation models, they only addressed the question of what form a change in preferences should take given a specific input, not *whether* any change should happen. We want to fill this gap, and for that purpose, we propose a connection between ranking preferences by how easily they change and whether change occurs. Why would one individual's preferences change when another individual's do not?

To formalise the problem, consider the story of Doyle and Paris. Our protagonists face a choice over what to study: physics or medicine. In the beginning, they share a strict preference for medicine over physics. Therefore, Doyle and Paris enrol in the medicine course. Full of excitement, they start their studies, learn numerous Latin names for bones, and have first patient contact. At this point, they both experience the tragic death of a patient. This experience has transformative potential and leads Doyle to undergo preference change. His preference between medicine and physics reverses. Doyle switches degrees. Paris has had precisely the same experience. However, this does not lead to a preference reversal in her case. She still prefers medicine over physics and is continuing her degree. Why did Doyle undergo preference reversal but Paris did not?

It seems that the difference between Doyle and Paris cannot be explained by new information learned from the patient's death.[38] They both knew that patients tragically die, and we can expect they had a good sense of how this

---

[37] One could also try to capture robustness differently. For example, one could define the robustness of a preference state regarding how persistent it is across changes in motivational reasons using reason-based decision theory. We thank Christian List for bringing this to our attention.

[38] We are not strictly required to deny that any readable information was acquired, only that any newly acquired information leads to derived preference change.

would feel. In essence, we stipulate that their experience brings no relevant information about either course of study. Nevertheless, their preferences might differ in stickiness, or so we suggest.

Crucially, Paris' preference is more robust than Doyle's despite them sharing relevant preferences and undergoing the same experience. A preference is more robust than another if, *ceteris paribus*, it takes a more intense experience to change it. A more intense experience is needed to override Paris' preference for medicine than Doyle's.

The story of Doyle and Paris undergoing a potentially preference-changing experience is just one example among many that our framework covers. As the following example illustrates, not all these experiences must be life-changing.

Rory and Jess prefer William S. Burrough to Ernest Hemingway, but they both read *The Old Man and the Sea* for school. While they have read it before on their own, the novel speaks much more to them on this occasion. They have an intense positive experience, despite receiving no new information about the book or its content.[39] This positive experience leads Rory to undergo motivational change. She now prefers Hemingway to Burrough, while Jess remains a Burrough fan.

Importantly, neither scenario can be covered by the approach of Hansson and Grüne-Yanoff, since the input-assimilation model always a priori assumes that preference change occurs. What is needed is a theory that connects the robustness to not only *how* preference change occurs but also *whether* it occurs. To fill this gap, we propose what we call the commitment-based theory of preference change.

The main idea of the commitment-based theory of preference change is that the robustness of an agent's preferences results from how committed they are to these preferences. Commitments are mental properties explaining motivational dynamics. In this way, commitment resembles entrenchment in the AGM modelling literature. Grüne-Yanoff and Hansson (2009) have also discussed such an entrenchment-inspired proposal but without taking the idea very far.[40]

We develop our framework for modelling these commitments in five steps:

---

[39] One proposal we do not discuss is that Rory and Jess might learn something new about themselves.

[40] Formally, the proposal briefly considered by Grüne-Yanoff and Hansson (2009: 179) resembles an ordinal version of our proposal, but they interpret it as second-order preferences and question whether such second-order preferences are stable enough to constrain preference change. We do not identify commitments with the intuitive interpretation of second-order preferences, insofar as we do not claim that the degree to which an agent wants to have a preference is the same as the degree of commitment to said preference. In fact, we would expect second-order preferences to influence commitments without being identical to them.

1. Presenting the basic assumptions about alternatives and preferences.
2. Outlining the newly introduced commitment function.
3. Developing our representation of experience.
4. Introducing the 'commitment-preservation identity' as a condition describing which preference ordering would result if an experience caused preference change.
5. Finally, introducing the intensity inequality that determines whether an experience is intense enough to cause this change.

Alternatives and Preferences

Our framework requires a set of alternatives and preference states held over these alternatives.[41] In the example of Doyle and Paris, the set of alternatives might simply be a set of available university courses:

$$A = \{\text{physics}, \text{medicine}, \dots\}.$$

For the purposes of our overview, we do not settle on the specific nature of the alternatives: they could be Savage-type consequences or Jeffrey-type propositions. However, we assume that A is the set of alternatives over which the fundamental preferences range. These fundamental preferences are taken to be well-described by a preference ordering that is represented as a set of preference states, P:

$$P = \{\text{medicine} \succ \text{physics}, \text{physics} \sim \text{physics}, \dots\}.$$

All preference orderings we consider will be complete, in that a preference state of strict preference or indifference holds between each pair of alternatives, including alternatives paired with themselves.

In our overview, we only consider preference changes in which agents replace indifference or strict preference between alternatives with the same two types of state. We will overlook other types of preference change, such as when a preference is withdrawn between two alternatives without indifference or a reversed preference takes its place, or when alternatives are lost or discovered.

Commitments and the Commitment Function

'Commitment' is used in many ways.[42] We add to this collection and use 'commitment' in a further technical sense: commitments determine the robustness of an agent's preferences in response to experiences. This general idea can be given two interpretations: strong and weak.

---

[41] The framework developed here is most easily interpreted using only strict preference and indifference.

[42] For some interesting uses of 'commitment', see Sen (1977) and Chang (2013).

In the strong interpretation, commitments are mental states that govern the robustness of preferences in the light of experiences. These mental states would have the function, presumably due to evolutionary selection, to ensure that preferences do not change haphazardly. If some process would affect a preference with strong commitment, the strong commitment state will act as a defence.

In the weak interpretation, commitments are just the robustness of preferences. According to this view, they are a dispositional property of preference states. Preferences are more or less fragile.

The two interpretations can be compared to two ways of explaining why a porcelain plate might not break during transport: either it has been packaged well in dampening materials, which are in this analogy equivalent to the commitment states, or it is not disposed to break, presumably due to its intrinsic properties. For the present purposes, we will not settle on one interpretation. In either interpretation, commitments to preferences are irreducible to the preference ordering, and our conditions can be applied to the dynamics of preferences.

While both Doyle and Paris initially prefer medicine to physics, they differ in their commitment to this preference. Importantly, their commitment is not reducible to the strength of their preference since it might be derived from their utility functions. That is, Paris being more committed to the preference for medicine over physics does not simply mean that the difference in utility between these two options is larger for her than for Doyle.[43] In our example, Paris and Doyle initially wanted to study medicine and physics to the same degree.

We do not consider the distinction between the strength and robustness of a preference to be particularly controversial once appropriately considered.[44] Fickle agents with strong desires (i.e. individuals who strongly want their preferred alternatives but nonetheless undergo substantial motivational change over time) are common. We have all heard of the fickle lover who desires with all their heart to be with the object of their love rather than anyone else, only to change their mind a day or two later. Their preference is strong but not robust.

The converse is also possible. Human agents exhibit anaemic but persistent preferences, which require intense experiences to be changed. A trivial example is a *ceteris paribus* preference for having $1010 rather than $1000 in one's bank account. Most of us would not be willing to do much to realise this preference. Yet, it would take an extremely intense experience, perhaps a conversion to a religion of poverty, to reverse this preference. The strength of preferences

---

[43] We assume here that utility functions are comparable between Doyle and Paris.

[44] The notion of strength used here should not be confused with the one used when distinguishing weak ($\succeq$) and strict ($\succ$) preference relations.

understood in terms of utility functions cannot account for such cases. Since robustness is distinct from strength, we postulate that commitment is distinct from desirability.

Based on this informal understanding, one can develop rigorous models that describe the role of commitment in preference change. However, there are multiple ways to develop such a framework. One key question is at which scale one should represent commitment. On an ordinal scale, commitments would only be taken to specify whether one preference is more robust than another but not how much more robust. A ratio scale allows such a specific comparison.[45]

Justifying a response to this question goes beyond what we can accomplish here. For the purpose of illustration, we will settle on a ratio-scale representation of commitment in the following since its power simplifies the presentation. However, at opportune moments, we will remark on how one could develop the framework differently.

Given the suggested representation of alternatives and preferences, commitments can be represented by a function from the set of preferences P to an appropriate interval. Specifically, we suggest that the function takes the form:

$$\text{com}: P \rightarrow \mathbb{R}.$$

For example, Paris' commitment might be 8 while Doyle's is only 6. We would write this as:

$$\text{com}_{\text{Paris}}(\text{medicine} \succ \text{physics}) = 8$$

$$\text{com}_{\text{Doyle}}(\text{medicine} \succ \text{physics}) = 6.$$

Intuitively, the higher the commitment to a preference relation, the more intrinsically robust the preference is (some special cases are treated in Appendix B). More precisely, we need to turn to the representation of experience.

Representing Experience

We have stipulated in our example that Doyle and Paris experienced the death of a patient in the same way, but one might inquire what it means for two experiences to be the same. It cannot be sufficient that the agents live through the same events because then a difference in how they interpret these events

---

[45] The ratio scale also requires a zero point, which will correspond to having a neutral experience in our framework. Looking at a white wall while thinking of something else is usually such an experience. If you do it too long, the boredom might develop an intensity, but a thoughtless glance will lack anything like it. Such a shared zero point will also enable an interpersonal comparison.

could explain the difference in preference change. Instead, it is required that the internal representation of the events is the same, at least insofar as the representation matters for the dynamics of preferences (cf. Bradley 2017: 185–86).

Experiences can be extremely rich and their processing highly complex, but we make the simplifying assumption that only two aspects of an experience matter for commitment-based preference change, which we call:

• Substantial component
• Intensity

First, an experience suggests changing particular preferences, and this suggestive part of the experience we call the 'substantial component'. For example, the substantial component of Doyle and Paris' experience suggests preferring physics over medicine, which can be represented as the singleton set {physics ≻ medicine}. The substantial component specifies which preferences are to be considered because of what has happened to the agent. This aspect of the experience mirrors the proposal by Hansson and Grüne-Yanoff, although we are not operating with general preference sentences.

Second, every experience has an intensity. Good experiences, such as enjoying a book by Hemingway, and bad experiences, such as witnessing a patient's death, have an intensity. We propose that the intensity of the experience can be represented by a real number on a ratio scale, meaning that such experiences can be more or less intense. In the case of Doyle and Paris, the experience is intense because it is highly tragic. In the case of Rory and Jess reading Hemingway, the experience is presumably of lower intensity.

As with the representation of commitment, one can – and should – question whether the intensity of experiences, such as the experiences of Doyle and Paris, is

1. representable by real numbers on a ratio scale;
2. whether intensities are commensurable across agents.

Defending these assumptions in all detail goes beyond the confines of our Element, and we will later outline how to model intensity on an ordinal scale instead. However, for now, we want to offer a potential path for approximately operationalising ratio-scale intensity.

The intensity of an experience might be approximated using the experience's degree of absolute pleasurability (i.e. treating both highly pleasing and highly displeasing experiences as intense and neutral experiences as lacking intensity).[46]

---

[46] This is a simplification since we do not want to claim that the intensity of every experience (e.g. mystical experiences) can be approximated solely by the experience's degree of pleasurability. The content and other features of the experience might make a difference, but this approach serves as a starting point for a preliminary empirical investigation.

Psychological research has provided evidence that experiences share a hedonic degree. For example, Kahneman (1999) proposes that *every* experience can be characterised by a value on a single good/bad dimension because the good experience of, for example, reading a book by Hemingway and the bad experience of the death of a patient share an attribute of goodness/badness. When the good/bad commentary is conscious, it is experienced as pleasure or distress, with a corresponding acceptance or rejection of the stimulus. If we determine the value of an experience affectively rather than cognitively (e.g. Zajonc 1980) and the affective evaluation works on pleasant/unpleasant dimensions (e.g. Kahneman 1999; Kauppinen 2015), the hedonic degree suggests itself as a proxy measure for intensity. Therefore, if two agents experience an event with the same intensity, they experience the same absolute hedonic degree. The intensity can then be represented by a function:[47]

$$I: E \rightarrow [0, \infty),$$

where E is the set of experiences, and the range starts at zero because it reflects the absolute hedonic degree (i.e. there is no negative intensity).

Accepting that intensity is on a ratio scale, an experience can be represented by an ordered pair with the substantial component (i.e. a set of preference relations suggested by the experience as the first member and the intensity as the second). For example, the experience of Doyle and Paris can be written as:

$$\langle \{\text{physics} \succ \text{medicine}\}, 7 \rangle.$$

The experience suggests a specific preference (i.e. to prefer physics over medicine), and it does so with a specific intensity.[48] That Doyle and Paris have the same experience means that the experience is correctly represented by the same tuple for our purposes. Both the substantial content and the intensity of the experiences are identical.

Condition 1: The Commitment-Preservation Identity

Given this formalisation of experiences, we propose that one equation specifies which preferences are changed if preference change occurs. The idea is simply that preferences are changed to minimise overall violation of commitments.

Assume an experience changes an agent's preferences. If Q represents the new preference ordering and $\mathbf{C}$ represents the set of all preference orderings

---

[47] Whether or not there is any finite ceiling on the intensity of experiences is an empirical question that this formalism leaves open.

[48] This formalism allows for one experience to suggest multiple preferences to be changed. For example, it could suggest that Doyle wants to go to another university in addition to switching programmes.

over the set of alternatives that are rational and compatible with the substantial component of the experience, then the identity is:

$$Q = \operatorname*{argmin}_{C \text{ in } \mathbf{C}} \left(\sum_{R \text{ in } P \backslash C} \operatorname{com}(R) \right).$$

This identity specifies that the new preference ordering is the one that is compatible with the experience and, at the same time, minimises the sum of violated commitments.[49] Specifically, the commitment-preservation identity requires that the new preference ordering is the ordering of $\mathbf{C}$ that minimises the commitment of preferences that must be abandoned (i.e. that are in P but not in Q). If the commitment to a preference state, R, is higher than others, it is less likely to be abandoned. Therefore, the identity selects the compatible preference ordering, minimising the commitment values of the preferences in the original but not the new preference ordering.

In the case of Doyle and Paris, the following two preference orderings might be amongst the candidates, one that only ranks physics over medicine and one that also ranks biology over medicine, where all preference states subsumed in the ellipses are identical:

1. {physics $\succ$ medicine, medicine $\succ$ biology, physics $\succ$ biology, ...}
2. {physics $\succ$ medicine, biology $\succ$ medicine, biology $\succ$ physics, ...}

If Doyle previously preferred both medicine and physics over biology and had positive commitments to these preferences, the first preference ordering would always have a lower overall violation of commitments. Therefore, it will be selected over the second candidate.

Interpreting the identity normatively, a rational agent *should* undergo preference change in such a way as to minimise the violations of commitments. Intuitively, a rational agent should not go overboard in accommodating an experience. In this regard, the commitment-preservation follows a similar motivation as Hansson and Grüne-Yanoff's model. However, there are important differences.

The most obvious difference is that our suggested model includes a ratio scale of commitment. However, one can also envision an ordinal version of our framework that could follow the model of Hansson and Grüne-Yanoff. That is, instead of requiring that the sum of the commitments be minimised, one can

---

[49] We assume here that the preference orderings are complete in the sense that between each two alternatives, either a strong preference or indifference holds. Otherwise one might want to also introduce a commitment to the absence of a preference.

require that as few preferences of the highest commitments be changed as possible, and then as few preferences as possible of the second tier, and so on.

A more profound difference is that in the Hansson and Grüne-Yanoff model, the revision operation specifies loosened alternatives and, thus, preferences that have priority when it comes to change. In our approach, commitments hold across preference transformations and determine the robustness of preferences. What is a property of the experience in their model is a property of the agent's cognitive system in ours. Despite starting with highly similar motivations, the variation in assumptions about what governs motivational dynamics leads to quite divergent models. The difference between them will become even more apparent with the second condition.

Condition 2: The Intensity Inequality

Having described *how* preferences change with the commitment-preservation identity, we propose that *whether* preference change occurs also depends on commitments. To capture this, we propose the inequality condition.

If $I(e)$ represents the intensity of an experience e and $\mathbf{C}$ represents the set of all preference orderings compatible with the substantial component of the experience, again represented using strict preference and indifference states, the inequality describing the condition under which preference change occurs is:

$$I(e) \geq \min_{C \text{ in } \mathbf{C}} \left(\sum_{R \text{ in } P \backslash C} \text{com}(R) \right).$$

Informally, preference change happens if and only if the intensity of the experience overcomes the sum of violated commitments. Therefore, we can describe the difference between Doyle and Paris. For Doyle, the intensity of the patient-death experience is greater than the sum of the commitments for the preferences that are abandoned. Put more informally: the experience hits him harder than the degree to which he hangs on to his preferences. Given that the experience is represented as $\langle \{\text{physics} \succ \text{medicine}\}, 7 \rangle$, we can write for Doyle:

$$7 \geq \min_{C \text{ in } \mathbf{C}} \left(\sum_{R \text{ in } P \backslash C} \text{com}(R) \right).$$

In contrast, for Paris, the condition is not fulfilled due to her greater commitment to the preference for medicine over physics:

$$7 < \min_{C \text{ in } \mathbf{C}} \left(\sum_{R \text{ in } P \backslash C} \text{com}(R) \right).$$

This formalism encompasses the examples of Doyle and Paris' life-changing experience and Rory and Jess' experience with Hemingway. In both examples, the agent who undergoes preference change fulfils the inequality condition, while the other does not.

Interpreting the inequality condition normatively, a rational agent should not change their preferences because they had a bad experience but because they also had a sufficiently intense experience. Interpreting the inequality condition descriptively, an agent will not undergo preference change whenever an adverse experience occurs, but they will if it is sufficiently intense.

The inequality condition requires the commensurability of the intensity of experiences with commitments for both its normative and descriptive tasks. Only then can we say that Doyle was hit harder by the experience than he was committed to his preferences. Accepting our story of Doyle and Paris, this claim appears natural to us.

To use the example of Shakespeare's Hamlet instead of our tale, assuming commensurability allows us to take at face value the following assertions: Hamlet's experience was more intense than his interest in society could withstand. While he strongly held social preferences before, never wavering in them, the experience was greater than them.

These assertions assume that Hamlet had persistent preferences to engage in social interaction over other activities and that these preferences were held to some degree. Furthermore, they assume the experience of his father's death and mother's remarriage to the murderer was greater than this degree. It is probably not the only way to read Shakespeare, but it seems intuitive enough to suggest that we have a grasp on the commensurability between experiences and commitment. Such a grasp, we suggest, arises from our acquaintance with similar situations.

These considerations appear to us sufficiently strong to provisionally base our model on this commensurability, albeit with the caveat that the overall model requires further empirical investigation.[50]

---

[50] To quantitatively compare experiences and commitments, an empirical approach might involve creating a numerical scale for both dimensions. For experiences, a survey could be developed to assess the intensity of individuals' experiences following specific events, with participants providing values on some scale. Similarly, for commitments, a study could gauge individuals' stability to their preferences, generating commitment values. However, it is crucial to acknowledge that obtaining accurate empirical measurements for experiences and commitments is very challenging.

Postulating and justifying commensurability between experience intensity and commitments is one thing; formalising this commensurability is another. To simplify this formalisation, we assume that both the commitment function and the intensity of an experience are on a shared ratio scale. For example, we assume that if an agent is twice as committed to a set of preferences, then the experience of changing these preferences also has to be twice as intense. Unlike an ordinal scale, the ratio scale can offer such a straightforward interpretation. We find it plausible, especially since we believe an experience can hit one person twice as hard as another and therefore have twice the impact.

Nonetheless, one could also develop an ordinal version of our proposal, which would preserve a more limited commensurability. For example, experiences could have a maximal commitment level that they can overturn. Therefore, one might explain why Paris' preference is more robust than Doyle's by:

1. postulating three levels of commitments to preferences: high, medium, and low;
2. ascribing a high commitment level to Paris' preference for medicine $\succ$ physics but a medium to low commitment level to Doyle's same preference.

Then, the experience ⟨{physics $\succ$ medicine}, medium⟩ would lead to a preference change for Doyle but not Paris.

This explanation does not require a full ratio scale. However, it still requires commensurability between intensity and commitment and between persons. Without the commensurability between persons, it would no longer be valid to assert that Doyle and Paris had the same experience since the intensity level of the experience would no longer be comparable.

If one went further and rejected the intrapersonal commensurability between intensity and commitment, the inequality condition could no longer be specified, even for one person. Therefore, the commensurability assumption is required even on the ordinal variant of our proposal.

The Commitment-Based Approach and Practical Rationality

In either the ratio scale or ordinal variant, the underlying motivation for the inequality condition is that an experience should not lead to preference change unless it is sufficiently intense. If every bad experience, such as suffering a paper cut while reading philosophy papers, makes one reconsider which university programme one prefers, the rational diachronic agency is lost. There is a need to restrict which experiences can cause preference change, and the commitment framework allows us to formalise this restriction. Notably, the motivations provided by Grüne-Yanoff transfer to our proposal:

1. The change process might have a cognitive cost; therefore, the less the preferences change, the lower the costs. Demanding sufficient intensity for preference change reduces the cost.
2. Insofar as existing preferences have been reached through investment and serve as cognitive capital, they should not be given up without need. In our model, the need is captured by the degree of intensity.
3. Preference change might also be limited so that preferences can fulfil their function in the life of human agents. Such stability will be increased if preference change follows the intensity inequality.

While the model of Hansson and Grüne-Yanoff does not include anything like intensity inequality, our proposal is supported by their motivations. The same underlying concern of how to accommodate practical rationality despite the occurrence of changing preferences drives the two modelling efforts. They also connect the modelling effort to less formal debates about practical rationality. At least two considerations offered in these debates further support the role of commitments as described by our model.[51]

First, commitments can help us to achieve our goals over time and to structure our lives. Therefore, they have instrumental value for us. In his 'planning theory', Bratman (1987) has, for example, argued that intentions are – in contrast to mere desires – future-directed and subject to specific rationality requirements. Intentions make it rational for us not to reconsider our plans in many situations and thus help us to deal with our limited resources and to overcome temptations (see Bratman 1995, 1998; Harman 1986; Holton 2004).

While Bratman's concept of 'intention' or Holton's concept of 'resolve' are not identical to our notion of 'commitment', the role they are ascribed and the rationality requirements are very similar. Such views are closely related to the 'paper-cuts argument': Diachronic rationality is lost when trivial events such as paper cuts frequently reverse consequential preferences, such as the one between fields of studies. An agent could never complete a multi-year course of studies if they constantly changed their mind. From Bratman and Holton to Hansson, Grüne-Yanoff, and us, the view is that preference change must be limited for preference states to fulfil their functions. Commitments are one way to meet this requirement.

Second, commitments can help us establish and maintain personal identity over time. For example, Paris' personal identity might involve a greater commitment to her course of study. In his later work, Bratman (2000, 2005) looks for states whose 'primary roles include the support of coordination by way of the constitution and support of connections and continuities, which, on

---

[51] We are grateful to Holger Baumann for providing valuable ideas for this section.

a broadly Lockean view, help constitute the identity of the agent over time' (Bratman 2000: 45). He identifies these states with 'self-governing policies', which are principles of action that structure our agency over time and ensure that we actively shape and maintain our identity. Again, this notion differs from our notion of commitment. However, the motivation is shared: the importance of commitments could be explained further by appealing to their role in our identity over time.

A similar view can be found in the work of Frankfurt (1982, 2006), who holds that acting on preferences or desires alone is insufficient for autonomous agency. According to him, such states are too fleeting and do not constitute the agent's own standpoint (Frankfurt 1999: 162). Instead, he proposes that states of 'caring' can play the agent's role. If an individual cares about something, they (1) have a stable disposition to act in certain ways, (2) are committed to what they care about (this includes feelings of frustration if they do not achieve it and active efforts to avoid such frustration), and (3) has a future-oriented outlook (e.g. Frankfurt 1982, 1999, 2006). This characterisation of caring is highly similar to commitments. The importance that we ascribe to commitments could thus be further supported by alluding to their contribution to autonomous agency: commitments might be said to constitute the agent's own standpoint, such that if they act according to their commitments, they act autonomously.

The Future of the Commitment-Based Approach

While we cannot develop the commitment-based approach at length, we hope it shows that many fruitful preference change models remain unexplored. The commitment-based approach starts from the idea that preferences differ in their robustness, which Hansson and Grüne-Yanoff have suggested, and we develop it considerably further by connecting it to the question of whether preference change occurs.

We have left many questions open, and to end this section, we pick one to show how an engagement with it could be of philosophical interest. The question is: what are the determinants of commitment? If commitment differs between individuals, we expect something to explain these differences. Innate personality traits, social pressure, and institutions might all affect our commitments. For example, the economic literature on endogenous preferences often relates the creation of preferences to social institutions (e.g. Bowles 1998; Poulsen and Poulsen 2006). From a philosophical perspective, exploring whether evidence on normative questions can change commitments would be especially interesting. For example, if one is convinced by the argument that lying is wrong, this experience might increase one's commitment to the relevant preferences. Similarly, if a friend with great musical taste suggests that the band Fugazi is aesthetically superior to Blink-182, one's commitment to this preference might grow stronger without the preference increasing in strength. As philosophers, we would like to know whether there are any normative or empirical restrictions on such commitment changes.

To address such questions, future philosophical work on preference change will increasingly need to engage with empirical results from cognitive science and psychology. Our outlined model indeed relies on such engagement since it is an open question whether agents have commitments governing preference change dynamics. That is not to say that such empirical explorations would be easy. In the case of commitment-based decision theory, it might require the ability to measure the intensity of experiences independently of preference change, a considerable challenge. Clever experimental designs are needed to show that complex models of preference change, such as the commitment-based model, can be considered an improvement.

The question of how to model preference change is not settled. However, having developed a better sense of the space of possible models, we can move to the next question: given that preferences will change, how can and should we choose as practical agents? If we have good reason to believe, perhaps due to a model, that a course of action might affect the preferences based on which we choose, should this alter our choice?

3 Rational Choosing in the Light of Change

Making rational decisions is difficult for many reasons. We are limited beings and might fail to consider the relevant utilities and probabilities of options (Kahneman and Tversky 2000). We might find it hard to compare the alternatives we face (Sartre 1957). Most importantly for our present topic, choosing may be difficult for us in light of preference transformations (Ullmann-Margalit 2006; Paul 2014; Pettigrew 2019). Especially in cases where we cannot even foresee the exact nature of coming preference change, our ability to choose rationally is questioned.

In this chapter, we discuss two debates in this context. First, we cover Laurie Ann Paul's (2014) approach in *Transformative Experience* and the recent literature on transformative experiences to which Paul's contribution gave rise. Second, we discuss Richard Pettigrew's proposal in *Choosing for Changing Selves* and the associated literature.

The Challenge of Transformative Experiences

Paul's *Transformative Experience* discusses whether some experiences transform us in such a way that we cannot rationally decide to undergo them as long as we exclusively base our decision on how much we will value these experiences. Examples of such experiences include having a first child or becoming a vampire. We are not the same afterwards, at least regarding our preferences.

In this context, Paul defines transformative experiences as experiences that are both epistemically and personally transformative. An epistemically transformative experience teaches you what it is like to be a certain way. For example, the experience of being a parent is the only thing that can teach you what it is like to be a parent, or so the example assumes.

A personally transformative experience changes your 'core preferences' (Paul 2014: 16). For example, being a parent likely changes your perspective on life and, by extension, your core preferences.[52] So, the choice of whether to have a child is a transformative decision since at least one of the available options (being a parent) leads to a transformative experience. We have already encountered another example of a transformative experience in the example of Doyle experiencing a patient's death while studying medicine. Further examples include:

- Switching careers
- Receiving a cochlear implant
- Undergoing gender reassignment surgery
- Moving to a new country
- Going to war
- Taking certain drugs

According to Paul, transformative decisions pose a fundamental problem for human agents because such choices cannot be rational in a specific decision-theoretic sense. As a first attempt, Paul argues that rationally choosing to become a parent, for example, requires knowing what it is like to be a parent and what one would value as a parent. However, one cannot know what this is like before becoming one.

Because there is some controversy on how to understand Paul's challenge to decision theory, we first focus on making it specific. Second, we reconstruct Paul's position regarding the challenge. Third, we provide a very brief overview of the current state of research focusing on decision-theoretic solutions aiming to overcome Paul's challenge.

---

[52] We have introduced a technical notion of 'fundamental preference' in Chapter 1. While we do not know what Paul exactly means by 'core preference', we believe that at least some of these core preferences will be fundamental in our sense.

The Challenge to Decision Theory

There are different ways to formulate Paul's challenge to decision theory and rationality more broadly understood.[53] Pettigrew (2015, 2020) argues that Paul challenges a deliberative conception of decision theory. According to the deliberative conception, an agent uses the decision-theoretic models to deliberate and make a rational choice according to their preferences. According to this conception, being rational means the deliberation preceding the choice fulfils certain rationality criteria. If you choose the best outcome without deliberating according to the formal decision theory framework, you are still irrational in the deliberative conception.

Transformative choices pose a problem for the deliberative conception of decision theory because they threaten the usefulness of decision-theoretic models for deliberation. Consider Paul's example of the decision of whether to have a (first) child. Applying Savage-type decision theory, one would proceed as follows.

First, one identifies the set of available actions. Let us suppose there are two options: having a child and not having a child (ignoring any difficulties regarding conception). Second, one assigns a utility to each potential outcome. The number of potential outcomes depends on the relevant states of the world. For illustration, assume that only the following states of the world matter for the decision: the relationship works out or falls apart, and one's financial situation is stable or unstable. Therefore, there are four relevant states of the world:

1. The relationship holds, and the financial situation is stable.
2. The relationship holds, and the financial situation is unstable.
3. The relationship falls apart, and the financial situation is stable.
4. The relationship falls apart, and the financial situation is unstable.

In this scenario, one determines the utility of eight potential outcomes (each action will lead to one of four different outcomes): the utility of having children given that the relationship holds and the financial situation is stable (Utility 1), the utility of not having children given that the relationship holds and the financial situation is stable (Utility 2), the utility of having children given that the relationship falls apart and the financial situation is unstable (Utility 3), and so on. We can express this as shown in Table 4.

Third, one multiplies each outcome's utility by how probable the state of the world is (i.e. one's level of confidence that the outcome will occur given the action) and calculates the EU of having a child and the EU of not having a child by adding up the utilities of the corresponding outcomes weighted by the subjective probability of the associated state of the world. Lastly, one chooses the action with the highest EU.

---

[53] For alternative proposals, see Campbell (2015), Chang (2015), Dougherty et al. (2015), Isaacs (2020), and Khan (2021).

Table 4 Decision whether to have a child

	Relationship holds		Relationship falls apart	
	Stable finances	**Unstable finances**	**Stable finances**	**Unstable finances**
Having a child	Utility 1	Utility 3	Utility 5	Utility 7
Not having a child	Utility 2	Utility 4	Utility 6	Utility 8

According to Paul, step 2 fails when the decision is transformative (Villiger 2021): one cannot even approximately assign any reliable utility to the outcome of having a child (Paul 2014: 19–23; 2015a: 3–5) because one does not have access to it (Pettigrew 2015). Denying any epistemic access raises the question of which notion of utility Paul presupposes.

Paul's concept of *subjective value* is crucial in this regard. While Paul (2014: 25) recognises that non-subjective values, such as objective moral and prudential values, can hold importance in some decisions, she sets them aside for the first-personal transformative choices of interest to her. Paul argues that even if the value of a non-phenomenal outcome can be evaluated, its unknown phenomenal value may be so positive or negative that it outweighs its known non-phenomenal value (Paul 2015c: 165 and footnote 4).

The centrality of subjective values in decision-making has been challenged (e.g. Chang 2015; Kauppinen 2015; Bykvist and Stefánsson 2017; Khan 2021). Bykvist and Stefánsson (2017) argue that assessing non-subjective values is crucial for agents who are not 'texture fetishists'. As defined by Bykvist and Stefánsson (2017: 131), texture fetishists are agents for whom the experience of an outcome largely determines its value.

The crucial aspect for us is the subjective aspect of experiencing or, as Campbell (2015) and Paul (2015b: 807) put it, living out the outcome, which ultimately determines its perceived value. With this in mind, we can draw upon the existing research in psychology to interpret Paul's understanding of utility.

Kahneman (2006) distinguishes between decision utility, experienced utility, and predicted utility.[54]

---

[54] According to Kahneman and Tversky (1984: 349), decision theory implicitly assumes that the so-called decision values and experience values coincide. The idea is that an ideal decision-maker (1) can predict future experiences perfectly and (2) can base the evaluation of the options on these predictions.

- Decision utility is equivalent to modern decision theory's concept of utility; it is the weight assigned to an outcome (Kahneman 2006: 489).
- Experienced utility is the positive or negative feeling corresponding to the chosen option. On a hedonistic interpretation, the experienced utility is the degree of pleasure or pain in the actual experience of an outcome, but other interpretations are possible.
- The predicted utility of an outcome is the agent's beliefs about the experienced utility at some future time.

Simplifying, we use Paul's concept of *subjective value* and the concept of experienced utility interchangeably. We do not mean to interpret Paul as a hedonist by this, but the notions of positive and negative feeling can be broadly construed as more than sensory pleasures and pain (e.g. a generally positive sense of having achieved one's goals).

Leaving experienced utility aside, predicted utility also plays a key role in Paul's examples: the prediction of one's experienced utility fails (at least, the prediction is not sufficiently reliable) because what she calls *cognitive modelling* fails.

On this reconstruction, Paul's challenge to deliberative decision theory can be understood as follows:

1. One does not have epistemic access to a transformative outcome's future experienced utility.
2. Therefore, it is impossible to determine the EU of a transformative choice.
3. Therefore, it is impossible to determine whether one prefers the transformative option (being a parent) or the non-transformative option (living a childless life).
4. Therefore, transformative decisions fall outside the realm of deliberative decision theory.

Reconstruction and Interpretation of Paul's Argument and Solution

In the previous section, we saw that there is a connection between Paul's work and the psychological literature on the gap between decision utility and experienced utility (i.e. mischoices in which we fail to choose the option that leads to the best experience) and the gap between predicted utility and experienced utility (i.e. mispredictions in which we fail to predict what will make us happy). Psychologists have described various causes for mischoices and mispredictions (see Buehler and McFarland 2001; Gilbert et al. 2002; Hsee and Zang 2006: 505):

- Agents might overlook important things.
- Agents might have incorrect beliefs.
- Agents over-predict external rewards, such as income.
- Agents underestimate intrinsic values, such as contact with friends.

Given this wealth of psychological research an agent could read, why does Paul claim that agents cannot access a transformative outcome's future experienced utility? According to her, the usual way one determines an outcome's utility is cognitive modelling, which she characterises as using a mental simulation to put oneself 'in the shoes' (i.e. the first-person perspective) of a future self. To determine what it would be like for oneself to have a child or to continue living without one, the agent creates a sort of mental cinema: 'In the first movie, one does have a child. In the second film, one lives a childless life' (Mathony and Messerli forthcoming: 2). Crucially, the agent not only imagines what they will do but also how the *experience* of being a parent would feel.

From Paul's viewpoint, the prescribed procedure of mental simulation is essential for the decision to be authentic. The notion of authenticity is integral to Paul's theory, and she would consider its abandonment highly unsatisfactory (Paul 2014: 112). Even if an agent were to know the transformative outcome's future experienced utility without undergoing mental simulation, the decision arrived at through such means would lack authenticity.[55]

However, in the case of transformative experiences, Paul argues that cognitive modelling fails (see Paul 2014: 124). As discussed earlier, such transformative experiences have a personal component insofar as they can change an individual's core preferences while simultaneously having an epistemically transformative component that puts up an 'epistemic wall'. According to Paul, we cannot penetrate this wall through imagination, testimony, or scientific investigation. One might think that scientific data could show what experiences result from becoming a parent. However, Paul argues that aggregated statistical data do not provide sufficiently fine-grained information on how one will experience having a child (Paul 2014: 131–32). She holds that the experience of being a parent only becomes accessible through becoming one.

When deliberating about whether to become a parent, one does not know, for example, one's career ambitions. As we understand Paul, the problem of personal transformation is, therefore, twofold:

---

[55] There are exceptions to this rule in Paul's view, such as in the case of getting one's legs amputated without anaesthesia. Even without a cognitive simulation, it is clear that amputation without anaesthetic would be a terrible experience for an agent. Every potential outcome of such a situation is negative, regardless of how specific those outcomes may be.

1. Do present preferences (e.g. career is more important than family) or future preferences (e.g. family is more important than career) matter more?
2. One does not know one's future, transformed preferences.

Therefore, there is not only the problem of whether current or future preferences should guide one's choice but also the problem that one's potential preferences after a transformative experience are inaccessible.[56]

In addition to raising the challenge, Paul offers her own solution: a rational agent should base transformative decisions on the so-called *revelatory value*. That is, instead of basing a transformative choice on a prediction regarding one's experienced utility, one should make such a decision by asking oneself how one values new experiences and new selves. According to Paul, we can rationally choose transformative experiences. However, such a choice requires resources not usually part of decision theory, such as a desire to undergo such experiences.

As part of her solution, Paul reformulates the structure of the decision problem so that the outcomes do not involve experiencing but rather discovering the transformative outcome. If you deliberate about epistemic transformative choices, such as trying durian fruit for the first time, the relevant outcomes are *discovering the taste of durian* and *avoiding discovering the taste of durian*. In Paul's view, these outcomes are independent of the experienced taste, which one cannot predict. Similarly, if you deliberate about personal transformative choices, such as being a parent for the first time or studying medicine, the crucial question is how much you value discovering what it is like to be a parent or a doctor: which Paul calls the *revelatory value*.[57]

However, it is questionable whether Paul's solution is successful. Some authors have claimed to spot tension in it (e.g. Kauppinen 2015; Shupe 2016; Bykvist and Stefánsson 2017). While Paul initially disregards non-phenomenal values such as those of prudence and morality and focuses on the issue of subjective values, she later proposes a solution that appears to be based on a non-phenomenal value: the revelatory value. As noted by Bykvist and

---

[56] Without epistemic transformation, one would know 'what's on the other side of the wall' and, as a result, the problem of personal transformation would be reduced to the still complex question of whether one should base one's decision on current or transformed (or maybe even past) preferences or some aggregate utility of them (e.g. Ullmann-Margalit 2006; Bykvist 2006; Pettigrew 2019). We will discuss this issue in the second half of this chapter.

[57] However, you also face a further challenge when confronted with a personal transformative choice: the preferences regarding the revelatory value might change. For example, before becoming a parent, you assign it a high revelatory value, and after the experience, a low revelatory value. However, Paul states that this challenge can be addressed: if you prefer to discover that your preferences change (independent of how they will change, which you do not know), you should choose the transformative option.

Stefánsson (2017), this presents a challenge for Paul since she must argue that the revelatory value is subjective despite facing difficulties in doing so.[58]

We provide an interpretation that identifies a related tension in Paul's solution, drawing upon prior research on this subject. Our argument has three steps.

First, as mentioned earlier, Paul proposes that a transformative choice should be taken authentically.

Second, for Paul, authenticity means 'authentic self-governance informed by knowledge via experiential or imaginative acquaintance with objects of deliberation' (Paul's characterisation of her concept of authenticity in her *Teaching Guide to Transformative Experiences*: 9; see also Paul (2015b: 807)). Note that Paul's perspective regarding what constitutes an authentic choice has thereby been subject to criticism.[59] As Khan (2021) noted, Paul posits that a transformative decision can only be deemed authentic if it involves mental simulation. Our interpretation aligns with Khan's (2021) assertion that Paul's definitions of rational and authentic preferences both entail imaginative acquaintance with potential outcomes (i.e. in Paul's view, an authentic choice necessitates cognitive modelling).

Third, the revelatory value is determined independent of forecasting/cognitive modelling in Paul's framework: one uses cognitive modelling to find out what an experience is like, but one does not use cognitive modelling to find out whether one wants to discover what the experience is like or to avoid discovering it. In other words, according to Paul, a choice based on the revelatory value does not involve cognitive modelling.

Therefore, a choice based on the revelatory value cannot be authentic. In summary, the tension is that Paul claims that a transformative choice should be taken authentically, but her own solution leads to the choice not being taken authentically. Therefore, Paul's solution appears unsatisfactory.

Addressing the Challenge

There remains a growing area of research on transformative experiences, with some philosophers accepting and some rejecting Paul's argument. We first point out views consistent with Paul's argument before turning to criticisms.

Arvan (2015) accepts Paul's conclusion that transformative choices fail to be rational. He argues that since we cannot know which major life choices are

---

[58] We are grateful to an anonymous reviewer for bringing to our attention this argument pertaining to Paul's solution.

[59] Campbell (2015) states that Paul's conception of authenticity is overly limited to the notion of 'knowing what it is like' and does not consider external or impersonal factors (see Paul (2015b) for a response). However, the objective here is not to evaluate Paul's definition of authenticity critically but to understand her perspective.

likely to be rational, we should train our capacity for resilience (i.e. a robust psychological disposition to respond adaptively to unexpected life events). Like Arvan, scholars who agree with Paul often connect transformative experiences with more applied topics.

Paul's contribution can also be viewed as intersecting with research on decision-making in situations of deep uncertainty (e.g. Karni and Vierø 2017; Helgeson 2020). Deep uncertainty occurs when agents cannot access complete information, the available present and future actions, the potential outcomes resulting from these actions, or the value associated with these outcomes. One interpretation of Paul's work considers it a philosophical addition to the discourse on decision-making with increasing awareness, where the decision-maker comprehends that the consequences currently beyond comprehension will become known upon implementation of the action.[60]

However, many philosophers disagree with Paul's challenge or think other solutions are available. We first highlight some *contra arguments*, which try to show that there is no actual challenge. Second, we present *decision-theoretic solutions* that attempt to address the presumed challenge.

Contra Arguments

One research branch asks whether imaginative projection is the only epistemic route available (see Dougherty et al. 2015; Cath 2019). Dougherty et al. (2015) propose that testimony and inference from similar experiences or behavioural observations can be used to estimate the value of new experiences. Therefore, they distinguish between the phenomenological character of an experience and its value. Their key point is that while one cannot know the phenomenological content of an epistemically transformative experience, its value can be known using the aforementioned methods. Similarly, Cath (2019) distinguishes two strategies for acquiring 'what it is like' knowledge. One way is to acquire it from a first-person perspective, via cognitive modelling, or, of course, from its actual experience. Another way is to acquire it from a third-person perspective, such as by consulting testimony.

A different branch of research critically examines the concept of cognitive modelling in greater detail (see Bykvist and Stefánsson 2017; Campbell and Mosquera 2020; Cath forthcoming). For example, Mathony and Messerli (forthcoming) provide empirical evidence on whether cognitive modelling fails for decisions likely to have transformative outcomes. They argue that cognitive modelling can be operationalised as affective forecasting, which is roughly our ability to predict the impact of certain experiences on our

---

[60] We thank an anonymous reviewer for bringing this to our attention.

happiness. More specifically, Mathony and Messerli compare transformative and non-transformative experiences relating to agents' ability to engage in affective forecasting. They find that decision-makers' performance in cognitively modelling transformative experiences does not systematically differ from that in cognitively modelling non-transformative experiences. According to Mathony and Messerli (forthcoming), individuals mispredict their future happiness levels at the same rate, regardless of whether the experience in question is transformative. If their operationalisation of cognitive modelling as affective forecasting, methodology, and meta-study results are sound, their conclusion directly opposes Paul's view on cognitive modelling and transformative experiences.

Decision-Theoretic Solutions

Many philosophers have presented their own choice models and solutions for how to rationally make transformative decisions (e.g. Campbell 2015; Kauppinen 2015; Pettigrew 2015, 2020; Reuter and Messerli 2018; Villiger 2021, forthcoming a, forthcoming b). We will discuss approaches by Reuter and Messerli (2018) and Pettigrew (2015, 2020), who have developed detailed decision-theoretical models to address Paul's challenge.

Multi-Criteria Decision-Making

Reuter and Messerli's (2018) approach is based on standard multi-criteria decision-making science (e.g. Ishizaka and Nemery 2013). The idea is that rational decision-making involves two components:

1. Value: the extent to which a criterion favours a certain outcome.
2. Weight: a criterion's relative importance.

To illustrate, imagine that you have to choose between buying one or another apartment, and suppose two criteria matter: price and location. First, each of the two criteria has a weight. If you consider both criteria equally important, their respective weights are 0.5. Second, both apartments have value regarding price and location. If one apartment is cheaper, it has a higher value regarding price. According to this approach, the overall utility of an action, such as buying an apartment, is determined by a weighted average of how much each criterion is fulfilled.

However, unlike standard multi-criteria decision science, Reuter and Messerli's approach allows decision criteria to be unknown. For example, you might not know whether you value one apartment more than another regarding location. This approach allows agents to form a preference ranking over acts even

Table 5 Multi-criteria decision-making

Criteria	Weight	Value for a child	Value against a child
Partner wants to have a child	0.40	1	0
Financial situation	0.35	0.5	0.5
Experienced utility of having a child	0.25	?	?

if values are unknown, for example, because they depend on the experienced utility of a transformative outcome.

To illustrate how the models work, we consider the transformative decision of whether to have a child. Assume that three criteria influence our agent's choice:

1. whether the agent's partner wants to have a child;
2. the agent's financial situation;
3. the experienced utility of what it is like to have a child.

Furthermore, these criteria differ in importance to the agent. The partner's opinion accounts for 40 per cent of the decision process ($w_{partner} = 0.4$), while financial impact contributes 35 per cent ($w_{financial} = 0.35$), and experience 25 per cent ($w_{experience} = 0.25$). For illustration, we assign the following values: $v_{partner/pro-child} = 1$ and $v_{partner/contra-child} = 0$ (i.e. the opinion of the partner speaks totally in favour of becoming a parent), $v_{financial/pro-child} = 0.5$, and $v_{financial/contra-child} = 0.5$. Notably, the experienced utility is unknown, so $v_{experience/pro-child} = ?$ And $v_{experience/contra-child} = ?$ A summary is provided in Table 5.

By calculating the overall utility for both acts – and only using the known weights and values – one arrives at:

$$U(\text{having a child}) = 0.4 \times 1 + 0.35 \times 0.5 = 0.575$$

$$U(\text{not having a child}) = 0 \times 0.4 + 0.35 \times 0.5 = 0.175.$$

Even if the experienced utility totally speaks against having a child (i.e. $v_{experience/contra-child} = 1$), the overall utility of not having a child would be at most $U(\text{not having a child}) = 0.425$ ($0.175 + 0.25$), which is still much lower than $U(\text{having a child}) = 0.575$. Therefore, preference ordering is possible, even if the experienced utility is unknown, provided $w_{experience} < 0.5$.

Of course, one might maintain that the weight $w_{experience}$ is generally >0.5. However, Reuter and Messerli (2018) conducted an empirical investigation asking individuals to weigh a range of values in terms of importance regarding questions such as whether or not to have a child. They found that the importance individuals assign to the weight $w_{experience}$ does not make it *impossible*, or even *improbable*, that they will form a rational decision and act towards what they prefer most. Indeed, because how an experience will feel does not have sufficient weight or, alternately, because other criteria are together sufficiently important, individuals faced with a transformative choice will make a rational decision much of the time.[61]

A more serious problem would arise if the weights could be changed due to the personally transformative character of the experience. If so, the weights assigned to what it will feel like to be a parent, for example, might increase so that an agent would have decided differently. Then, the decision would have arguably failed to be rational. Put simply: the worry is that the weights might also be outcome-dependent. However, the empirical data that Reuter and Messerli (2018) have collected from individuals who already have children (and, therefore, have already had the transformative experience and the possibly changed weights) are relatively robust (i.e. the weights of the decision criteria look similar to those who had not undergone the experience).

Reuter and Messerli's solution has been criticised on both theoretical and empirical grounds. One theoretical critique refers to the fundamental assumptions of multi-criteria decision-making models. Most such models assume (a) the separability of the decision criteria (to avoid double-counting); (b) the numerical ascertainability of the criteria weights; (c) the value and weight attributions range between 0 and 1; and (d) that for each criterion, $v_{outcome\ 1} + v_{outcome\ 2} = 1$ (e.g. $v_{experience/contra-child} + v_{experience/pro-child} = 1$). Assumption (c) is particularly controversial (see Villiger (forthcoming b)) for a critique. For instance, why can values not be >1? The reason is that values can be taken to represent whether a criterion is fulfilled in multi-criteria decision-making models. For example, if one's partner wants to have a child, the respective criterion is fulfilled ($v_{in\ favour\ of\ child} = 1$).

One justification for imposing a normalisation on values can be found in the satisficing theory (Simon 1955). While there are significant differences between the satisficing and multi-criteria decision-making models, Simon's rationale for

---

[61] It might sound implausible that a choice can be rational even though it occurs in the context of a misprediction of one's experienced utility. However, this is sensible when other values are at stake that are independent of experience prediction. Reuter and Messerli (2018: 27–28) have conducted a *permutation test* that suggests such independence.

satisficing can also be extended to multi-criteria decision-making: the classical conception of rationality embodied in standard decision theory is overly demanding demands on decision-makers. A normalised multi-criteria approach is easier for us as limited human beings to handle.[62]

Villiger (forthcoming b) also argues that Paul's challenge explicitly refers to Savage-type EU theory. However, it is unclear why one must stick to this version of decision theory. After all, the important question is which theory is more plausible for deliberation. Crucially, Paul seems to accept Reuter and Messerli's theoretical choice model for making rational transformative decisions (Chituc et al. 2021).

Instead, Chituc et al. (2021) criticise Reuter and Messerli (2018) on empirical grounds. They argue that the so-called *evaluability bias* explains Reuter and Messerli's empirical findings. The idea is that participants attach more weight to the decision criteria they can know, and since they cannot know $w_{experience}$, they attach less weight to it.[63] While the evaluability bias might indeed play a role in explaining participants' responses, we should remember that a preference ordering in Reuter and Messerli's model is possible as long as $w_{experience}$ < 0.5. Furthermore, more research is needed regarding the normative relevance of the objection (is the evaluability bias always irrational?) and the relationship between subjective and non-subjective values in general (how should a decision-maker weigh experiential values relative to non-experiential values?).

Uncertain Utilities: The Fine-Graining Solution

According to Reuter and Messerli's choice model, a transformative decision can be rational even when the experienced utility of a transformative outcome is *unknown*. In contrast, Pettigrew's choice model is based on the idea that the experienced utility of a transformative outcome can be *known* to a certain degree.

Pettigrew's (2015, 2016, 2019, 2020) *Fine-Graining Solution* responds to Paul's challenge by building uncertain utilities into EU theory. Since one does

---

[62] To better reflect the observable behaviour of human agents in light of these limitations, Simon (1955: 104) proposes several simplifications and modifications, one of which involves categorising possible consequences into two groups: satisfactory (1) and unsatisfactory (0). This approach notably resembles assumption (c) in multi-criteria decision-making models.

[63] Chituc et al. (2021) agree with Reuter and Messerli that participants attach little weight to the subjective value compared to the other decision criteria. Moreover, they replicated Reuter and Messerli's rank ordering of the relevant decision criteria. However, they argue that participants care about subjective value even if they attach less weight to it. Chituc et al. also present empirical evidence that participants attach less weight to subjective value because it is difficult to evaluate, not because it is unimportant.

Table 6 The fine-graining solution

Group A	P(having children | U(having children) = 2)	0.4
Group B	P(having children | U(having children) = 4)	0.6

In this case, the expected value for having children is 3.2 ($0.4 \times 2 + 0.6 \times 4$).

not know the utility of having children, one instead uses expected values for the utility of having children. That is, one replaces the utility of having children with more fine-grained expected values for having children using testimony from those who already have children.

Let us assume that parents fall into two groups. According to Group A (let us say 40 per cent), the utility of having children is 2. According to Group B (the remaining 60 per cent), the utility of having children is 4. We can express the probabilities derived from this situation as in Table 6.

Pettigrew's solution circumvents the problem of a transformative outcome's inaccessible future utility value by making the utility value part of the outcome (i.e. fine-graining). Evidently, the utility of the outcome 'becoming a parent and the utility of becoming a parent is 2' is 2, regardless of whether becoming a parent is transformative. In Pettigrew's approach, EU doubly depends on the agent's degrees of belief.

Given the important role such degrees of belief play within Pettigrew's approach, they deserve their own discussion. Paul (2014, 2015a, 2015b) and Pettigrew (2015, 2016, 2019) have debated the question of whether evidence from other individuals (i.e. those who already have children) does sufficiently concern one's own utility. As already mentioned, Paul claims that an authentic self bases their evidence on knowledge via experiential or imaginative acquaintance. In Pettigrew's view, statistical evidence about other individuals' utilities tells one something about one's own utilities.

Consider an agent with certain character dispositions who lives in specific social conditions and has an intrinsic desire to become a parent. Suppose individuals in Groups A and B were sufficiently similar to our agent when they decided to become parents. In this case, the expected value of 3.2 for having children tells our agent something about their EU of having children.

Another issue raised in the literature is the interpersonal comparability of utility. Isaacs (2020) criticises Pettigrew's approach because averaging across different utility functions does not work with so-called 'cardinal utilities'. Without going into detail, the idea is that we cannot compare the utilities and, therefore, we cannot even group individuals according to their utility as demonstrated in Table 6. Instead, additional information is required to compare the utilities of different agents. For example, we would need to know that value X of one individual utility function is the same as value Y for another function. Therefore, according to Isaacs (2020), Pettigrew's solution presupposes a more enriched concept of utility than cardinal utility.

There are at least two ways to address the problem of comparability. First, an approach that replaces utility with expected values for utility need not presuppose testimony and thereby avoid comparisons between agents. Second, some formal approaches build on Pettigrew's solution but try to avoid the problem of interpersonal utility comparisons. For example, Villiger (2021) argues that due to fundamental higher-order facts that apply to any type of experience, an agent at least knows the general shape of the utility space.[64]

Pettigrew has proposed a solution to Paul's challenge, but he goes beyond transformative experiences. His work concerns the general question of whether an agent should base their choice on current, future, or past preferences, a question to which we also now turn.

The Challenge of Changing Selves

Anne and John have always dreamed of starting a family. They have been in a loving relationship for several years; so they discuss whether to finally have a child. Anne currently wants to continue travelling around the world with John. However, Anne believes it is quite likely that if she had a baby, she would prefer having the child and settling down. That is, Anne's future self, as a mother, would probably prefer having settled with a baby over travelling.[65]

Anne faces a crucial problem: if she chooses to have a child, her future preferences (settling down is preferable over travelling) presumably replace her current preferences (travelling is preferable over settling down). On which preference should Anne base her choice?

Drawing upon Pettigrew's *Choosing for Changing Selves* (2019), we call this the *challenge of changing selves*. We present three potential solutions to this

---

[64] Pettigrew (2019: 102–103) presents an additional solution that enables utility comparisons. However, note that Pettigrew's solution primarily addresses the question of how an individual can compare their various selves' utilities over time. Since selves will resemble each other over time, this is an easier problem than interpersonal utility comparison in general. Pettigrew (2019: 97) defends this assumption by stating that, 'my future self has a good deal more insight into the mind of my past selves than I have into your mind or the minds of even my close friends and family'. Of course, one might object that according to Pettigrew's Parfitean metaphysics, the relevant notion of being the same or a different person can be graded on a spectrum and that this also applies to interpersonal utility comparisons.

[65] For the sake of simplicity, we largely ignore the option of travelling with a baby, even though some individuals are choosing it and live accordingly.

challenge. The first solution states that Anne should base the decision only on her present preferences. The second solution states that Anne should base the choice on her higher-order preferences (Ullmann-Margalit 2006). However, most of our attention will be given to a third solution advanced by Pettigrew (2019), who argues that Anne should base her choice on a weighted average of past, present, and possible future preferences.[66]

Present Preference Solution

Isaacs (2020: 1074) claims that Anne's change of preferences is not problematic since decision theory does not depend on future utilities. He writes, 'It is easy to say what an agent should do in the face of potentially changing utilities – maximise EU relative to his current credences and current utilities' (Isaacs 2020: 1078).[67] In Isaacs' view, current Anne should prevent future Anne from getting what she wants if what she wants is diametrically opposed to what current Anne wants.[68] Therefore, Anne should continue travelling without having a baby.

One way to elaborate is to argue that rational choice is limited to an individual's current preferences and beliefs because standard decision theory aims to formalise means-end rationality. According to this view, it is not means-end rational to choose means to attain goals that the agent has discarded or has not yet embraced. However, note that a means-end interpretation is not universally accepted since decision theory does not necessarily involve an instrumental conception of practical rationality (e.g. Nida-Rümelin 1994).

Another way to elaborate is to argue, like Paul, that we cannot predict our own future preference changes (e.g. Elster 1983).[69] Consequently, present preferences are all Anne has when making a choice. This response suggests that Anne simply has no idea whether her future preferences will diverge from her current ones. For example, Anne cannot predict whether her future self will enjoy settling down with a baby more than travelling. After all, a significant percentage of individuals regret parenthood (e.g. Donath 2015; Geißler and

---

[66] One might also argue that Anne should base her choice only on future preferences. For example, Schulz (2020) can be interpreted this way.

[67] Isaacs (2020) does not provide a crafted argument for why only present preferences matter because this is not the main point of his paper.

[68] Parfit (1984) holds a similar view, claiming that future goals do not matter for present choices.

[69] Note that Elster's view is more complex and particularly relevant in the context of so-called *adaptive preference change*. According to Elster (1983: 117), one type of adaptive preference change is not intended but is rather a causal process that merely happens to oneself. Therefore, the change in preferences is not rational (for an opposing view, see Bruckner (2009)). However, Elster (1983: 25) also argues that adaptive preference change can be rational when preferences are changed intentionally through character planning.

Laude 2016), and some individuals travel with babies. Furthermore, preferences may change unexpectedly even if Anne chooses the non-transformative option. Anne's desire to travel may weaken or disappear even if she tries to avoid transformation.

While some uncertainty is to be expected, humans nonetheless seem able to base their choices on possible future preferences and anticipate them to a certain extent. The idea that preference change can be foreseen is especially plausible if – contrary to Paul – one considers testimony and that one's values are socialised (i.e. created through socialisation processes). In Anne's case, consulting testimony could be informative.

Geißler and Laude (2016) stated that approximately one-fifth of parents regret parenthood. Assuming that nothing about Anne renders her especially similar to these regretful parents, she would most likely not regret the choice to have a child. Therefore, she can somewhat confidently predict the probability distribution of her future preferences and could reasonably act upon them.

A further option to justify the present preference solution would be to argue that our present preferences already appropriately consider our future preferences, or at least should do so. When Luke realises that his future self will prefer to retire and go fishing instead of continuing to work, this might change Luke's present preferences for future retirement, perhaps even his current preferences regarding how much money to save each month. Our present preferences are not causally independent from our beliefs regarding our future preferences. Provided the present and future self are appropriately related to each other, considering each other in their standard preferences, there is no need to consider more than the present preferences. Otherwise, the future preferences would just be accounted for twice.

However, it seems to us that sometimes agents disagree, even conflict, with their future selves. Luke might resent his future self for wanting to go fishing rather than continue the working lifestyle he currently values. He might even save less money to ensure his future self cannot fulfil its preference. While such extreme cases of disagreement might be less common, it seems to us that more than the present preference solution is needed to address them.

Higher-Order Preference Solution

Ullmann-Margalit (2006) proposes that Anne should base her choice on higher-order preferences (preferences over preferences). To illustrate the concept of higher- and lower-order preferences, consider Frankfurt's (1971: 8) example of a drug addict. A drug addict might have a first-order preference to consume drugs instead of abstaining but a higher-order preference not to have the preference to consume drugs.

According to Frankfurt's (1971: 7) view, Anne's ability to reflect on her preferences allows the formation of higher-order preferences. When confronted with a choice that might lead to a change of some preferences, Anne should therefore ask herself which of these preferences she would prefer to have: does she want to become the person that prefers having a child or remain the person that prefers travelling (Ullmann-Margalit 2006: 167)?[70]

Advocates of a higher-order preference solution have to address at least two challenges. First, the *normativity challenge* concerns the normative power of higher-order preferences and questions whether higher-order preferences are worthier than first-order preferences. The second challenge highlights that higher-order preferences can also change: Anne's higher-order preference for settling down might reverse when she experiences motherhood. We call this the *higher-order change challenge*. We briefly discuss both challenges, beginning with the normativity challenge.

One possible response to the normativity challenge is to assert that low-order preferences backed up by higher-order preferences typically promote an agent's well-being more than those lacking such backing. This promotion of well-being would then justify giving them priority.

There are two problems with this argument. First, it is questionable whether there are objective facts about what is valuable for each comparison of goals or preferences (Pettigrew 2019: 47). For example, it seems dubious that there is an objective fact regarding whether studying business administration is more valuable than studying art.[71] Second, it is questionable whether lower-order preferences backed up by higher-order preferences necessarily promote an agent's well-being more. While this may be true in the case of Frankfurt's drug addict, it might be false in the case of Anne. It is entirely possible that Anne has a higher-order preference for a first-order preference for being a mother and that the satisfaction of this preference will decrease her well-being. Indeed, there is empirical evidence that parents' levels of life satisfaction decrease on average and stay below their previous childless levels of life satisfaction for

---

[70] Ullmann-Margalit (2006) also suggests that Anne should take small steps to ensure the continuity of her personality over time. She illustrates this with the following example: 'Thus, if the big decision you face is whether to marry this man or not, you may try to arrange for the two of you to live together for a while so that you can get a foretaste of your future life – and of your future self – as his spouse' (Ullmann-Margalit 2006: 169). While this is (often) a reasonable strategy, note, however, that Anne is almost at the point of no return in our case. One cannot try out a child like a new outfit, or at least one should not. And while spending time with nephews and nieces might be advisable before making a decision, one can question whether it is really the same as having a child of one's own.

[71] See Pettigrew (2019: chapter 5) for an overview and serious objection to the proposal that Anne has one so-called true utility function.

several years (e.g. Luhmann et al. 2012). One may interpret this as evidence that parents' well-being decreases on average.

Another argument is that only higher-order preferences reflect who we want to be and what we consider meaningful. In this view, Anne's higher-order preference for becoming a mother reflects what she considers a meaningful life. However, this approach is also controversial. Assume that Anne becomes extremely unhappy as a settled-down mother who does not perceive her parental duties as meaningful. In this case, the preference for settling down with a child over travelling might be backed up by a higher-order preference – she would prefer to have such a preference – but it is unclear whether acting on this preference reflects what is more meaningful to Anne.

In addition to the questions about the normative force of higher-order preferences, the higher-order change challenge looms. If future higher-order preferences differ from current ones, how should we choose between them? Pettigrew (2019: chapter 4) seems correct that the higher-order preference solution, which he calls 'the Utility of Utility Solution', does not solve the challenge of changing selves but pushes the problem to a higher-order level. Why should Anne prioritise present higher-order preferences rather than possible future higher-order preferences?

Therefore, it is clear that both the present and higher-order preference solutions face problems. Nevertheless, Anne's preferences will likely change when she gets older, regardless of which option she chooses. Therefore, Anne must face the challenge of how to choose in light of future preferences that likely differ from her current ones.

Pettigrew's Aggregate Utility Solution

Pettigrew's (2019) aggregate utility solution is based on the idea that Anne's past, present, and future selves can be treated as a group of individuals whose attitudes must be aggregated. In other words, Anne is a collective entity comprising diverse selves whose attitudes must be aggregated. While Anne's current self is making a choice, she must decide on behalf of all three selves since each self contributes to the person Anne. So, when Anne decides, she should base her choice not only on her present utilities but also on those of her past and possible future selves matter, although to different degrees.[72] From this metaphysical perspective, Pettigrew can use social choice theory tools to address the problem of choosing to change selves.[73]

---

[72] The idea that each self's value over time matters can also be found in Bykvist (2006).

[73] Bykvist (2021) critically discusses whether Pettigrew's metaphysical perspective justifies the interpretation of an agent's decision-making challenge as analogous to a social choice problem.

Of course, much is to be said about how exactly this aggregation will be modelled, and many options exist. For example, one could use majority voting instead of Pettigrew's weighing scheme. In light of this universe of options, Pettigrew spends much effort justifying his exact aggregation model, but we will limit ourselves to presenting the final results of his theory. The key points can be summarised as follows:

- The aggregation occurs on the levels of utilities and subjective probabilities (rather than preferences or beliefs, for example).
- The aggregation takes the form of a weighted average. That is, the final value function should average the utility function of each relevant self, weighted by how much that self's mental state should matter.
- To determine the weights, Pettigrew makes recourse to Derek Parfit's contribution to ethics and the personal identity debate. In particular, the degree of connectedness between individuals plays a role in specifying the average's weights.

Applying this strategy, Pettigrew would argue that Anne should base her choice on a weighted average of past, present, and potential future utilities. This weighted average should then determine the evaluation of acts and inform her decision.

To illustrate how Pettigrew's solution works, we ignore uncertainty and just ask how Anne should calculate the utilities for the outcome of settling down with a child over a life of travelling. In this case, Anne should proceed in two steps to make a rational choice.

In the first step, Anne determines the utilities of the outcomes: the extent to which her past, current, and future selves value this choice, multiplied by the weights assigned to the respective selves. Simplifying, by only taking one future self into account, for now, we can represent this as follows:

- Past Anne's utility in future Anne settling down with a child: $U_{Past}(\text{settling down})$
- Current Anne's utility for the same future option: $U_{Present}(\text{settling down})$
- Future Anne's utility: $U_{Future}(\text{settling down})$

The indices concern the utility of which self is considered, while the option is always considered to be in the future.

Our case study, in which future Anne would prefer having a baby but current Anne would prefer travelling, indicates that: $U_{Present}(\text{settling down}) < U_{Present}(\text{travelling})$. Nonetheless, it might be the case that the future self assigns a larger utility to settling down: $U_{Future}(\text{settling down}) > U_{Future}(\text{travelling})$. This relation

Table 7 Aggregate utility solution

	Settling down	Travelling
U_{Past}	2	1
U_{Present}	1	2
U_{Future}	2	1

might be shared by the past self so that U_{Past}(settling down) $>$ U_{Past}(travelling). After all, Anne and John have dreamed of starting a family.

A situation like this can be summarised as shown in Table 7 if we assign utilities to how Anne's selves evaluate the corresponding outcome.

To signify that these different utilities add up to one individual's utility, we have the weights for them add up to 1. For illustration: if the weight of current Anne's utility is 0.6 and the weight of future Anne's utility is 0.3, then the weight of past Anne's utility is 0.1.

Using these weights, U_{Overall}(settling down) would be $0.1 \times 2 + 0.6 \times 1 + 0.3 \times 2 = 1.4$ and U_{Overall}(travelling) would be $0.1 \times 1 + 0.6 \times 2 + 0.3 \times 1 = 1.6$. In this scenario, the overall utility for settling down turns out to be smaller, but we have only considered one future Anne so far. There might very well be a second possible future Anne that assigns U_{Future}(settling down) $= 5$. Assuming that the future Anne's split the overall weight of the future and keeping all other utility assignments identical, we arrive at U_{Overall}(settling down) $= 0.1 \times 2 + 0.6 \times 1 + 0.15 \times 2 + 0.15 \times 5 = 1.85$.

In the second step, Anne should calculate which act maximises her EU. At this stage, we could reintroduce uncertainty (i.e. Anne would have to multiply the overall utilities of the outcomes with the respective probabilities that the outcomes will occur). Since this step would follow the procedure of Savage-type decision theory, we will not describe it again.[74]

Thus far, we have illustrated how aggregation, including weights, works.[75] How to determine the weights is another question. Pettigrew follows Parfit and accepts that *connectedness* is more important than *personal identity* and

---

[74] However, one might raise the question of whether only the present degrees of belief or also past and future degrees of belief should be taken into account. Should utility and probability functions be treated the same or is there a difference between their roles that justifies treating them differently? We do not further pursue this question to focus on the change of preferences.

[75] Simplifying the discussion, we have glossed over crucial issues, such as *cross-world interventions*, for example. A cross-world intervention occurs when, for example, Anne's decision-making utility in one possible world affects her utilities in another possible world. Pettigrew's aggregation procedure excludes such interventions, and Pettigrew acknowledges that others, such as Bykvist (2006), have also done so.

sympathises with the following principle: the more connected a self is to Anne's present self, the more the weight that should be attached to it.

The crucial question for us is what *being connected* means when applied to different selves. Pettigrew makes three claims. First, Anne's past self is connected to her present self in that Anne now benefits from her past sacrifices. One can imagine, for example, that Anne previously saved money and worked hard to later be in a good position to have a child. According to Pettigrew (2019: 172), Anne is therefore obliged to give a certain amount of weight to her past self.

Second, Anne is cognitively connected to her various selves, in that they share experiences and cognitive states, such as memories and beliefs. Following Parfit, Pettigrew (2019: 187–192) argues that these cognitive connections are a legitimate reason to discount the future; the weaker the cognitive connection between a future self and Anne's current self, the less the weight that should be given to that future self.

Third, Anne is connected to her selves, in that they share values; therefore, the closer the self's values are to Anne's current values, the more the weight that should be assigned to them (Pettigrew 2019: 213). In other words, the more similar Anne's different selves' utilities are to her present self's utility, the higher the weight it should be assigned. In Pettigrew's view, agents feel less alienated the more they base their decisions on commonly shared values. To illustrate this idea, consider a student who does not value money but studies business instead of art because they expect to care about money in the future. If our student despises individuals who consider money important but nevertheless assigns a great weight to their potential future self, they will feel alienated.

The aggregate utility solution seems to be a more promising approach than the present or higher-order preference solution. Nonetheless, we will briefly hint at two concerns: *unknown past utilities* and *constraints on weights*.

Regarding the first concern, it is helpful to recall that the challenge of transformative experiences not only consists of the question of whether present or future values matter more but also of the fact that one does not know one's future values. Therefore, Anne does not know her future self's utility of having a child. Pettigrew proposed the fine-graining technique as a solution (see the 'Uncertain Utilities – The Fine-Graining Solution' section). Applied to our example, this means that future Anne's utility can be replaced by the aggregate of the utilities of Anne's several possible future selves. In this way, Pettigrew offers a method to address unknown future utilities. However, he underestimates that one might not know one's past utilities either. The main reason past utilities might be unknown is that memory is unreliable and often inaccurate.

In the context of this debate, the episodic memory of what an experience was like and how one valued it seems to be crucial. Let us call the memory of what an experience was like 'qualitative memory' (Montero 2020) and the memory of how one valued what it was like 'evaluative memory' (Kahneman 2006). For example, remembering that giving birth was painful differs from remembering how the pain felt. Both qualitative and evaluative memory are problematic in their own ways, but qualitative memory is especially so. While mothers remember that they felt pain during childbirth, they often cannot remember how this pain felt.

To give a more mundane example, consider the rollercoaster ride experience. If one had a perfect qualitative memory of this experience, one would only need to experience it once. To experience the thrill of a rollercoaster ride again, one could simply remember the already-experienced ride. Luckily for rollercoaster operators, recalling qualitative memories is not so simple: one must go for another ride. However, it is not only qualitative but also evaluative memory that is flawed (Kahneman 2006). If this is true (i.e. past utilities cannot be remembered accurately), it is questionable whether Anne can make an intertemporal and, in a way, interpersonal utility comparison between her past, present, and future selves (see Ahmed 2021b: 485–87).

In response, Pettigrew might question whether imperfect memory is a problem specific to his solution. He could argue that the problem of imperfect memory applies to all relevant forms of decision theory. Let us again consider the rollercoaster example to illustrate this idea. In order to know whether one should prefer a rollercoaster ride to a museum visit, one needs to assess the two different experiences. For this, one must typically either have experienced such a ride to assess its utility value or be able to ask others who have experienced the ride. While in some cases there might be other evidence, such as based on scientific investigations, usually somebody must have had the experience and know about it. Consequently, if nobody accurately remembers how they valued the experience, the option's utility value cannot be assessed, and decision theory does not help us choose. While this would be a disappointing outcome for decision theory (and sounds slightly absurd), it is not a criticism specific to Pettigrew.

Another option would be for Pettigrew to propose using retrospective expectations. Just as in the case of the future, agents would consider multiple epistemically plausible past versions of themselves.[76] However, this attempted solution might appear to neglect an important difference between past and future, at least from the perspective of an agent about to choose: only one past has occurred to them, while many future paths appear open. Why should pasts matter that are not

---

[76] We thank an anonymous reviewer for drawing our attention to this option.

even actual options anymore?[77] Some of the standard arguments for EU, where we also use expectations, might be applicable, but not straightforwardly, if at all.

Any such justification must address the fact that some of Pettigrew's (2019: 169) reasons for considering the past, such as to account for past effort, appear to depend on only considering the actual past. The past effort in achieving a degree matters when deciding whether to stay in university now because it was actually spent, not because it could have been spent. Otherwise, Anne would have to consider all the effort spent by a possible past Anne to become a mother!

Pursuing this argument further, if only one case matters, is then expectation really the best way to consider the past? This question may be addressed, but as of yet, it points to a gap in the aggregate utility solution.

The second concern relates to the constraints on weights. According to Pettigrew (2019: 159), there are few strict rationality constraints on how an agent should weigh their past, present, and future selves. However, one might worry whether the weights will end up determinate enough to allow changing selves to choose rationally. To achieve determinacy, Pettigrew explicitly goes beyond the rationality requirements of decision theory and considers a more general notion of *reasonable* weights.

Introducing the concept of reasonable weights is a further step away from traditional decision theory than providing formalism for accounting for past and future preferences. Preferences are at least the type of objects that usually have their home in decision theory, while the considerations that Pettigrew now brings into the discussion do not. For example, in decision theory, we do not typically accuse individuals who abandon their present values of having 'sold out' (Pettigrew 2019: 210–211) or believe that morally better options should get higher weight (Pettigrew 2019: 35–36).

While allowing to assign more specific weights, introducing such broadly moral considerations also invites further controversy. Can Anne only rationally choose to have a child after reflecting on her ethical obligations to her future self? Is a strong moral anti-realist unable to rationally choose as a changing self? In light of such issues, one might hesitate to introduce moral considerations into a theory of how instrumentally rational agents whose preferences change should choose.

We have outlined the two concerns in broad terms only to showcase active areas of engagement. Much remains to be said on both Pettigrew's approach and the challenge of choosing to change selves in general.

---

[77] However, depending on one's metaphysics of time, the future might also be already settled. But from the perspective of an agent facing a decision, this is not the case. Their choice appears to them to make a difference. We will not further consider issues of free will in this case.

While we cope daily with changes in what we want, appearing to act as practical agents that broadly realise their preferences, our theories of how we face the problem of choosing to change selves are heavily debated and will remain so for the foreseeable future. We do not need a theory of knowledge to know, and we do not need a complete account of practical agency to be practical agents. However, when faced with troubling decisions and the prospect of changing preferences, it would at least provide some peace of mind if we could refer back to well-developed and well-founded theories of our agency. We hope our discussion of the various debates has made progress towards this purpose. Since your authors strongly prefer changing their minds in light of new arguments, we look forward to further developments in these debates.

Conclusion

Because preference change figures in various philosophical debates, it has invited a wide range of perspectives. For example, some philosophers adapt the standard decision theory tools by extending Bayesian conditioning or preference logic. Other philosophers inquire into the very source of preference change (e.g. reason-based decision theory). A third group of researchers is primarily driven by the problems preference change poses for us as practical agents in the world, the work of Pettigrew and Paul being prime examples. While we have not synthesised all these accounts – loose strands still point to future research directions – we have attempted to reduce the distance between debates.

Specific threads can be discerned in the literature, one of which we have particularly emphasised at various points in our discussion: preference change is assumed to be a cognitively real phenomenon and has to be treated as such. Due to this realism, models of preference change have to reflect real cognitive processes.

The model of Hansson and Grüne-Yanoff was motivated by the cognitive role of preferences. Therefore, empirical results about this role can substantiate or undermine their account. Our own model of commitment-based preference change can only be considered a hypothesis until the proposed dynamics of change have been observed. In addition, even the debate of transformative experiences, which is mostly normative rather than descriptive, relies on understanding preference change as a real phenomenon.

Reviewing the literature, a need for engagement with empirical research into human cognition becomes apparent. If we want to describe our practical agency or prescribe its functioning, we have to develop empirically adequate models of our psychological realisation of it. Preference change plays a rich role in agency, and an interdisciplinary effort is required to answer the philosophical questions it raises. We hope to have provided the philosophical foundations for success in such collaborations.

Appendix A
More on Fundamental and Derived Preferences

As discussed in chapter 1, Jeffrey-type decision theory does not have a notion of fundamental preferences by default. Bradley has provided a way to introduce a distinction between fundamental and derived preferences into the Jeffrey framework by specifying a subset of all alternatives that are considered fundamental. In his proposal, Bradley formalises propositions as subsets of a set of possible worlds, $\Omega = \{\omega_1, \omega_2, \ldots\}$ (i.e. the proposition that the university is disposed to accept your application would be the set of worlds in which this proposition is true). Then, the fundamental desirabilities are those assigned singleton subsets from this set (i.e. $v(\omega_1)$ being the desirability for one possible world).[78] The desirabilities across possible worlds are more fundamental, in that the desirabilities of all other propositions can be mathematically derived from them.

If we accept this notion of fundamental preferences, the invariance of fundamental desirability can be written as (see Bradley 2009: 228):

$$v^*(\omega) \geq v^*(\omega') \leftrightarrow v(\omega) \geq v(\omega'),$$

where v^* is the desirability function after a change, and v is the preceding function. Given the known connection between desirability functions and preferences, the invariance of preferences is also guaranteed:

$$\omega \succcurlyeq^* \omega' \leftrightarrow \omega \succcurlyeq \omega',$$

where $\succcurlyeq^*$ represents the preference relation after a change and $\succcurlyeq$ represents the preceding one. For example, one would expect this invariance to hold in the lottery ticket case. To generally assert this principle is to deny preference change.

Our proposal of mentally fundamental preference states does not have these preferences range over possible worlds. Therefore, one might ask the following question: does a further refinement of the alternatives (i.e. a refinement of the partition) change them?[79] To make this challenge more specific, imagine an

---

[78] We are also using the name of a world (e.g. ω_1) to represent the singleton set only containing this world (e.g. $\{\omega_1\}$). For more on the relation between possible worlds and propositions as objects of decision theory, see Bradley (2017: chapter 8, especially p. 130).

[79] We thank Richard Bradley for pressing us on this point. Any misconceptions are entirely due to us.

agent with the preferences A $\succ$ B $\succ$ C for the three propositions *A*, *B*, and *C*, which are each true for some non-singleton set of possible worlds. For the sake of this example, we use the following correspondence:

- A: $\{\omega_1, \omega_2, \omega_3\}$
- B: $\{\omega_4, \omega_5\}$
- C: $\{\omega_6, \omega_7\}$

That is, proposition A is true in the worlds ω_1, ω_2, ω_3, and so on for B and C.

The agent might then be presented with options in terms of possible worlds instead (i.e. they are to choose between disjunctions of singleton sets, including disjunctions corresponding to A, B, and C). Will this redescription of options lead them to exhibit different preferences regarding A, B, and C? That is, will the agent in response exhibit, for example, the preferences: $(\omega_6 \vee \omega_7) \succ (\omega_4 \vee \omega_5) \succ (\omega_1 \vee \omega_2 \vee \omega_3)$, or some other permutation diverging from A $\succ$ B $\succ$ C? Neither an affirmative nor a negative answer seems appealing.

A positive answer (i.e. one endorsing that such change occurs) would suggest that these supposedly mentally fundamental preferences (A $\succ$ B $\succ$ C) are not fundamental after all. Simply changing the description of the alternatives changes them.

However, a negative answer also appears to cast doubt on whether these preferences are truly fundamental because then it seems that these coarser preferences can just be derived from the more refined ones. It is as if the agent had always followed their finer preferences over possible worlds.

We hold that by distinguishing descriptive and normative decisions, one can defuse the problem of refining the partition of alternatives. Consider the first option of affirming change: when it comes to descriptive decision theory, we do not see a problem with accepting that presenting the agent with more fine-grained choices can lead to a change in fundamental preferences (and therefore derived preferences). As should be clear, we endorse the reality of preference change, and redescription appears to be a quite plausible cause of such change.

However, there is a better case for rejecting the first option when it comes to normative decision theory. As Bradley writes, 'The mere fact that one's attitudes are defined on a domain that has proved to be too coarse does not give one any reason to change one's attitude to the coarse-grained prospects themselves' (Bradley 2017: 257). In effect, Bradley appeals to a principle of minimal change so that preferences should only change if one's experiences or other reasons support doing so. If one accepts such a principle of minimal change, then normative decision theory would speak against the first option.

Regarding the second option, we must again distinguish between the descriptive and normative cases. Descriptively, one might doubt that an agent can maintain the same preferences at a higher level when confronted with a finer partition. However, the result is then just a preference change, and we return to the first option as a solution.

On a normative construal, the second option appears less problematic. To return to the principle of minimal change mentioned earlier, it might be the case that agents should have fundamental preferences that remain the same, even after fine partitions were introduced. However, these invariant preferences do not imply that the possible finer preferences are the true fundamental preferences. In this case, the agent appears to have had finer preferences, but appearance is not everything. From the mentalist perspective, what matters is which preference states are realised in the agent's mind. There are good reasons, such as space constraints, to assume that agents do not realise preferences over all possible worlds; instead, the normative constraint would be that *newly* formed preferences cohere with those held for the previous partition.

Therefore, we conclude that the first option appears plausible and acceptable from the perspective of descriptive decision theory, while the second option appears more acceptable from the perspective of normative decision theory, at least if one endorses a version of the principle of minimal change. Either way, the existence of fundamental preferences over alternatives coarser than possible worlds is defensible, and we can assume it for our analysis of fundamental preference change.

Appendix B
Special Cases for Commitment

In this appendix, we cover two special cases regarding commitments:

- Preferences that cannot be lost
- Negative commitment

The first special case is preferences that are so sticky that one cannot lose them. For example, a rational agent cannot lose the indifference between studying physics and studying physics (i.e. the preference state physics $\sim$ physics). There are multiple options for dealing with these preferences in the commitment function (e.g. assigning them an infinite commitment). However, the commitment value of such preferences can be left undefined, and instead, one can restrict the candidate preference orderings appropriately. If one requires that all preference orderings in **C** fulfil the agent's rationality criteria, all of them will include the preference physics $\sim$ physics, assuming reflexivity of indifference is among the criteria.

The second special case is negative commitments. Such commitments cover cases where preferences are only held to maintain rationality, given other preferences. Assume that Paris prefers studying medicine to physics and is indifferent between physics and biology. Assume also that she is highly committed to these preference states. For example, she has the following commitments:

$$\mathrm{com}(\mathrm{medicine} \succ \mathrm{physics}) = 10$$

$$\mathrm{com}(\mathrm{physics} \sim \mathrm{biology}) = 10.$$

Accordingly, transitivity (specifically, what is known as PI-transitivity) requires that Paris also prefers medicine to biology. However, it might very well be the case that she would not do so if it were not for this demand of rationality. In this case, she might have a negative commitment:

$$\mathrm{com}(\mathrm{medicine} \succ \mathrm{biology}) = -1.$$

That is, she would give up this specific preference if it were not for other preferences that, together with the constraint of rationality, force her to maintain it. Also giving up the other preferences to maintain rationality is also unappealing, given her strong commitments to them. In summary, negative commitments account for cases in which rationality and other commitments force agents to adopt a preference they would otherwise give up.

The strength of a negative commitment would indicate the degree to which an agent strains to get rid of it. The other preferences creating the rationality requirement would also need to be held with stronger commitment to outweigh the negative commitment.

That said, while our formalism allows negative commitments to exist, this does not commit us to their empirical existence. If one finds them unintuitive despite the aforementioned example, one can postulate a psychological law that agents have a minimal commitment to their preferences. The example of Paris would then be taken care of without needing negative commitments.

References

Ahmed, A. (2021a). *Evidential Decision Theory*, Cambridge University Press.

Ahmed, A. (2021b). *Choosing for Changing Selves*, Richard Pettigrew. Oxford: Oxford University Press, 2019, xiv 253 pages. *Economics & Philosophy*, 37(3), 484–500.

Alchourrón, C. E., Gärdenfors, P. & Makinson, D. (1985). On the logic of theory change: Partial meet contraction and revision functions. *Journal of Symbolic Logic*, 50(2), 510–30.

Alechina, N., Liu, F. & Logan, B. (2013). Minimal preference change. In D. Grossi, O. Roy & H. Huang, eds., *Logic, Rationality, and Interaction. LORI 2013. Lecture Notes in Computer Science, vol. 8196*. Springer, pp. 15–26.

Angner, E. (2018). What preferences really are. *Philosophy of Science*, 85(4), 660–81.

Arvan, M. (2015). How to rationally approach life's transformative experiences. *Philosophical Psychology*, 28(8), 1199–218.

Binmore, K. (2008). *Rational Decisions*, Princeton University Press.

Bowles, S. (1998). Endogenous preferences: The cultural consequences of markets and other economic institutions. *Journal of Economic Literature*, 36(1), 75–111.

Bradley, R. (2007). The kinematics of belief and desire. *Synthese*, 156(3), 513–35.

Bradley, R. (2009). Becker's thesis and three models of preference change. *Politics, Philosophy and Economics*, 8(2), 223–42.

Bradley, R. (2017). *Decision Theory with a Human Face*, Cambridge University Press.

Bradley, R. & Stefánsson, H. O. (2017). Counterfactual desirability. *The British Journal for the Philosophy of Science*, 68(2), 485–533.

Bratman, M. (1987). *Intention, Plans, and Practical Reason*, Harvard University Press.

Bratman, M. (1995). Planning and temptation. In L. May, M. Friedman & A. Clark, eds., *Mind and Morals: Essays on Ethics and Cognitive Science*. MIT Press, pp. 293–310.

Bratman, M. (1998). Toxin, temptation, and the stability of intention. In J. Coleman & C. Morris, eds., *Rational Commitment and Social Justice: Essays for Gregory S. Kavka*. Cambridge University Press, pp. 59–83.

Bratman, M. (1999). *Faces of Intention: Selected Essays on Intention and Agency*, Cambridge University Press.

Bratman, M. (2000). Reflection, planning, and temporally extended agency. *The Philosophical Review*, 109(1), 35–61.

Bratman, M. (2005). Planning agency, autonomous agency. In J. Taylor, ed., *Personal Autonomy*. Cambridge University Press, pp. 33–57.

Bratman, M. (2007). *Structures of Agency: Essays*, Oxford University Press.

Bridges, D. S. & Mehta, G. (1995). *Representations of Preferences Orderings*, Springer.

Bruckner, D. (2009). In defense of adaptive preferences. *Philosophical Studies*, 142(3), 307–24.

Buehler, R. & McFarland, C. (2001). Intensity bias in affective forecasting: The role of temporal focus. *Personality and Social Psychology Bulletin*, 27(11), 1480–93.

Bykvist, K. (2006). Prudence for changing selves. *Utilitas*, 18(3), 264–83.

Bykvist, K. & Stefánsson, H. O. (2017). Epistemic transformation and rational choice. *Economics and Philosophy*, 33(1), 125–38.

Bykvist, K. (2021). *Choosing for Changing Selves*, by Richard Pettigrew. *Mind*, 130(520), 1327–36.

Cadilhac, A., Asher, N., Lascarides, A. & Benamara, F. (2015). Preference change. *Journal of Logic, Language and Information*, 24(3), 267–88.

Campbell, J. (2015). L. A. Paul's transformative experience. *Philosophy and Phenomenological Research*, 91(3), 787–93.

Campbell, T. & Mosquera, J. (2020). Transformative experience and the shark problem. *Philosophical Studies*, 177(11), 3549–65.

Carel, H. & Kidd, I. J. (2020). Expanding transformative experience. *European Journal of Philosophy*, 28(1), 199–213.

Cath, Y. (2019). Knowing what it is like and testimony. *Australasian Journal of Philosophy*, 97(1), 105–20.

Cath, Y. (forthcoming). Transformative experiences and the equivocation objection. *Inquiry*, 1–22.

Chang, R. (2013). Commitment, reasons, and the will. *Oxford Studies in Metaethics*, 8, 74–113.

Chang, R. (2015). Transformative choices. *Res Philosophica*, 92(2), 237–82.

Chituc, V., Paul, L. A. & Crockett, M. (2021). Evaluating transformative decisions. *Proceedings of the Annual Meeting of the Cognitive Science Society*, 43, 973–78.

Cohen, M. D. & Axelrod, R. (1984). Coping with complexity: The adaptive value of changing utility. *American Economic Review*, 74(1), 30–42.

Davidson, D., McKinsey, J. C. C. & Suppes, P. (1955). Outlines of a formal theory of value, I. *Philosophy of Science*, 22(2), 140–60.

de Jongh, D. & Liu, F. (2009). Preference, priorities and belief. In T. Grüne-Yanoff & S. O. Hansson, eds., *Preference Change: Approaches from Philosophy, Economics and Psychology.* Springer Netherlands, pp. 85–107.

Dietrich, F. & List, C. (2013a). A reason-based theory of rational choice. *Noûs,* 47(1), 104–34.

Dietrich, F. & List, C. (2013b). Where do preferences come from? *International Journal of Game Theory,* 42(3), 613–37.

Dietrich, F. & List, C. (2016a). Mentalism versus behaviourism in economics: A philosophy-of-science perspective. *Economics and Philosophy,* 32(2), 249–81.

Dietrich, F. & List, C. (2016b). Reason-based choice and context-dependence: An explanatory framework. *Economics & Philosophy,* 32(2), 175–229.

Donath, O. (2015). *Regretting Motherhood—A Study,* North Atlantic Books.

Dougherty, T., Horowitz, S. & Sliwa, P. (2015). Expecting the unexpected. *Res Philosophica,* 92(2), 301–21.

Elster, J. (1983). *Sour Grapes: Studies in the Subversion of Rationality,* Cambridge University Press.

Fishburn, P. (1991). Nontransitive preferences in decision theory. *Journal of Risk and Uncertainty,* 4(2), 113–34.

Frankfurt, H. (1971). Freedom of the will and the concept of a person. *The Journal of Philosophy,* 68(1), 5–20.

Frankfurt, H. (1982). The importance of what we care about, reprinted in H Frankfurt (1988), *The Importance of What We Care about,* Cambridge University Press, pp. 80–94.

Frankfurt, H. (2006). *Taking Ourselves Seriously & Getting it Right,* Princeton University Press.

Frankfurt, H. (1999). On caring. In H. Frankfurt, ed., *Necessity, Volition, and Love.* Cambridge University Press, pp. 155–80.

Geißler, H. & Laude, S. (2016). *Regretting Parenthood: Ursachen und Demografie bereuter Elternschaft,* YouGov.

Gilbert, D. T., Wilson, T. D. & Driver-Linn, E. (2002). The trouble with Vronsky: Impact bias in the forecasting of future affective states. In L. F. Barett and P. Salovey, eds., *The Wisdom in Feeling: Psychological Processes in Emotional Intelligence.* Guilford Press, pp. 114–43.

Girard, P. (2008). *Modal logic for belief and preference change.* Unpublished PhD thesis, Stanford University.

Grüne-Yanoff, T. (2013). Preference change and conservatism: Comparing the Bayesian and the AGM models of preference revision. *Synthese,* 190(14), 2623–41.

Grüne-Yanoff, T. & Hansson, S. O. (2009). From belief revision to preference change. In T. Grüne-Yanoff & S. O. Hansson, eds., *Preference Change: Approaches from Philosophy, Economics and Psychology.* Springer, pp. 159–84.

Guala, F. (2019). Preferences: Neither behavioural nor mental. *Economics & Philosophy*, 35(3), 383–401.

Gustafsson, J. E. (2010). A money-pump for acyclic intransitive preferences. *Dialectica*, 64(2), 251–57.

Gustafsson, J. E. (2013). The irrelevance of the diachronic money-pump argument for acyclicity. *Journal of Philosophy*, 110(8), 460–64.

Hansson, S. O. (1995). Changes in preference. *Theory and Decision*, 38(1), 1–28.

Hansson, S. O. (2001). *The Structure of Values and Norms*, Cambridge University Press.

Hansson, S. O. & Grüne-Yanoff, T. (2017). Preferences. In E. N. Zalta, ed., *The Stanford Encyclopedia of Philosophy*. Stanford University. https://plato.stanford.edu/entries/preferences/.

Harman, G. (1986). *Change in View: Principles of Reasoning*, MIT Press.

Hausman, D. M. (2012). *Preference, Value, Choice, and Welfare*, Cambridge University Press.

Helgeson, C. (2020). Structuring decisions under deep uncertainty. *Topoi*, 39(2), 257–69.

Hole, B. & Selman, L. (2020). Illness as transformative experience: Implications of philosophy for advance care planning. *Journal of Pain and Symptom Management*, 59(1), 172–77.

Holton, R. (2004). Rational resolve. *The Philosophical Review*, 113(4), 507–35.

Hsee, C. & Zhang, J. (2006). Distinction bias: Misprediction and mischoice due to joint evaluation. In S. Lichtenstein & P. Slovic, eds., *The Construction of Preference*. Cambridge University Press, pp. 504–31.

Isaacs, Y. (2020). The problems of transformative experience. *Philosophical Studies*, 177(4), 1065–84.

Ishizaka, A. & Nemery, P. (2013). *Multi-Criteria Decision Analysis: Methods and Software*, Wiley.

Jeffrey, R. C. (1990) [1965]. *The Logic of Decision*, 2nd ed., University of Chicago Press.

Kahneman, D. & Tverksy, A. (1984). Choices, values and frames. *American Psychologist*, 39(4), 341–50.

Kahneman, D. (2006). New challenges to the rationality assumption. In S. Lichtenstein & P. Slovic, eds., *The Construction of Preference*. Cambridge University Press, pp. 487–503.

Kahneman, D. (1999). Objective happiness. In D. Kahneman, E. Diener & N. Schwarz, eds., *Well-Being: The Foundations of Hedonic Psychology.* Russell Sage Foundation, pp. 3–25.

Kahneman, D. & Tversky, A. (2000). *Choices, Values and Frames*, Cambridge University Press and the Russell Sage Foundation.

Karni, E. & Vierø, M. (2017). Awareness of unawareness: A theory of decision making in the face of ignorance. *Journal of Economic Theory*, 168(C), 301–28.

Kauppinen, A. (2015). What's so great about experience? *Res Philosophica*, 92(2), 371–88.

Khan, S. (2021). Rational preference in transformative experiences. *Synthese*, 199(3), 6715–32.

Kreps, D. (1988). *Notes on the Theory of Choice*, Routledge.

Levine, L., Lench, H., Kaplan, R. & Safer, M. (2012). Accuracy and artifact: Reexamining the intensity bias in affective forecasting. *Journal of Personality and Social Psychology*, 103(4), 584–605.

Lichtenstein, S. & Slovic, P. (2006). The construction of preference: An overview. In S. Lichtenstein & P. Slovic, eds., *The Construction of Preference*. Cambridge University Press, pp. 1–40.

Liu, F. (2010). Von Wright's 'The Logic of Preference' revisited. *Synthese*, 175(1), 69–88.

Luhmann, M., Hofmann, W., Eid, M. & Lucas, R. E. (2012). Subjective well-being and adaptation to life events: A meta-analysis on differences between cognitive and affective well-being. *Journal of Personality and Social Psychology*, 102(3), 592–615.

Mathony, M. & Messerli, M. (forthcoming). Transformative experiences, cognitive modelling and affective forecasting. *Erkenntnis*.

Melville, H. (1951). *Moby-Dick; or, The Whale*, Richard Bentley.

Montero, B. (2020). What experience doesn't teach: Pain amnesia and a new paradigm for memory research. *Journal of Consciousness Studies*, 27(11), 102–25.

Nida-Rümelin, J. (1994). Rational choice: Extensions and revision. *Ratio*, 7(2), 122–44.

Parfit, D. (1984). *Reasons and Persons*, Oxford University Press.

Paul, L. A. (2014). *Transformative Experience*, 1st ed., Oxford University Press.

Paul, L. A. (2015a). Transformative choice: Discussion and replies. *Res Philosophica*, 92(2), 473–545.

Paul, L. A. (2015b). Transformative experience: Replies to Pettigrew, Barnes and Campbell. *Philosophy and Phenomenological Research*, 91(3), 794–813.

Paul, L. A. (2015c). What you can't expect when you're expecting. *Res Philosophica*, 92(2), 149–70.

Pettigrew, R. (2015). Transformative experience and decision theory. *Philosophy and Phenomenological Research*, 91(3), 766–74.

Pettigrew, R. (2016). Book review of L. A. Paul's Transformative Experience. *Mind*, 125(499), 927–35.

Pettigrew, R. (2019). *Choosing for Changing Selves*, 1st ed., Oxford University Press.

Pettigrew, R. (2020). Transformative experience and the knowledge norms for action: Moss on Paul's challenge to decision theory. In E. Lambert & J. Schwenkler, eds., *Becoming Someone New: Essays on Transformative Experience, Choice, and Change*. Oxford University Press, pp. 100–21.

Poulsen, A. & Poulsen, O. (2006). Endogenous preferences and social-dilemma institutions. *Journal of Institutional and Theoretical Economics*, 162(4), 627–60.

Quinn, W. S. (1990). The puzzle of the self-torturer. *Philosophical Studies*, 59(1), 79–90.

Rachman, S. & Arntz, A. (1991). The overprediction and underprediction of pain. *Clinical Psychology Review*, 11(4), 339–55.

Reuter, K. & Messerli, M. (2018). Transformative decisions. *The Journal of Philosophy*, 115(6), 313–35.

Samuelson, P. A. (1938). A note on pure theory of consumer's behaviour. *Economica*, 5(17), 61–71.

Sartre, J.-P. (1957). Existentialism is a Humanism. In W. Kaufmann, ed., *Existentialism from Dostoevsky to Sartre*. Meridian, pp. 287–311.

Savage, L. J. (1954). *The Foundations of Statistics*, Wiley in Statistics.

Schulz, M. (2020). Uncertain preferences in rational decision. *Inquiry*, 63(6), 605–27.

Sen, A. (1986). Behaviour and the concept of preference. In J. Elster, ed., *Rational Choice*. Basil Blackwell, pp. 60–81.

Sen, A. (1993). Internal consistency of choice. *Econometrica*, 61(3), 495–521.

Sen, A. K. (1977). Rational fools: A critique of the behavioral foundations of economic theory. *Philosophy & Public Affairs*, 6(4), 317–44.

Shupe, E. (2016). Transformative experience and the limits of revelation. *Philosophical Studies*, 173(11), 3119–32.

Simon, H. A. (1955). A behavioral model of rational choice. *The Quarterly Journal of Economics*, 69(1), 99–118.

Spohn, W. (2009). Why the received models of considering preference change must fail. In T. Grüne-Yanoff & S. O. Hansson, eds., *Preference Change: Approaches from Philosophy, Economics and Psychology*. Springer Netherlands, pp. 109–21.

Stigler, G. J. & Becker, G. S. (1977). De Gustibus Non Est Disputandum. *The American Economic Review*, 67(2), 76–90.

Tahko, T. E. (2018). Fundamentality. In E. N. Zalta, ed., *The Stanford Encyclopedia of Philosophy*. https://plato.stanford.edu/archives/fall2018/entries/fundamentality/.

Thoma, J. (2021). In defence of revealed preference theory. *Economics & Philosophy*, 37(2), 163–87.

Tversky, A. (1969). Intransitivity of preferences. *Psychological Review*, 76(1), 31–48.

Ullmann-Margalit, E. (2006). Big decisions: Opting, converting, drifting. *Royal Institute of Philosophy Supplements*, 81(58), 157–72.

van Benthem, J. & Liu, F. (2007). Dynamic logic of preference upgrade. *Journal of Applied Non-Classical Logics*, 17(2), 157–82.

van Benthem, J. (2009). For better or for worse: Dynamic logics of preference. In T. Grüne-Yanoff & S. O. Hansson, eds., *Preference Change: Approaches from Philosophy, Economics and Psychology*. Springer Netherlands, pp. 57–84.

Velleman, D. (1989). *Practical Reflection*, Princeton University Press.

Villiger, D. (2021). A rational route to transformative decisions. *Synthese*, 199(5–6), 14535–53.

Villiger, D. (forthcoming a). The role of expectations in transformative experiences. *Philosophical Psychology*.

Villiger, D. (forthcoming b). Rational transformative decision-making. *Synthese*.

Vredenburgh, K. (2020). A unificationist defence of revealed preferences. *Economics & Philosophy*, 36(1), 149–69.

Vredenburgh, K. (2021). The economic concept of a preference. In C. Heilmann & J. Reiss, eds., *The Routledge Handbook of Philosophy of Economics*. Routledge, pp. 67–82.

Walsh, E. (2020). Cognitive transformation, dementia, and moral weight of advance directives. *The American Journal of Bioethics*, 20(8), 54–64.

Warren, C., McGraw, P. & Van Boven, L. (2011). Values and preferences: Defining preference construction. *Wiley Interdisciplinary Reviews: Cognitive Science*, 2(2), 193–205.

Wilson, T. D., Wheatley, T., Meyers, J. M., Gilbert, D. T. & Axsom, D. (2000). Focalism: A source of durability bias in affective forecasting. *Journal of Personality and Social Psychology*, 78(5), 821–36.

Zajonc, R. (1980). Feeling and thinking: Preferences need no inferences. *American Psychologist*, 35(2), 151–75.

Acknowledgements

We would like to thank Richard Bradley, Richard Pettigrew, Daniel Villiger, Holger Baumann, Luca Barlassina, Robert Stern, and Christian List for their helpful comments on individual parts of the book and earlier versions of ideas presented herein. We also thank the audiences at the Dortmund Work-in-Progress Group, the Taiwan Metaphysics Colloquium, and Peter Schaber's Research Colloquium, where this work was presented. We also greatly appreciate the support of the editor, Martin Peterson. The anonymous reviewers' criticisms were extremely valuable for improving the book's quality. Finally, we thank C. McElroy and T. Pemberton for their professional proofreading. The open access fee has been paid by the Swiss National Science Foundation (10BP12_222494). Michael Messerli was funded by an SNF Ambizione Grant [PCEFP1_186151].

Cambridge Elements ≡

Decision Theory and Philosophy

Martin Peterson
Texas A&M University

Martin Peterson is Professor of Philosophy and Sue and Harry E. Bovay Professor of the History and Ethics of Professional Engineering at Texas A&M University. He is the author of four books and one edited collection, as well as many articles on decision theory, ethics and philosophy of science.

About the Series

This Cambridge Elements series offers an extensive overview of decision theory in its many and varied forms. Distinguished authors provide an up-to-date summary of the results of current research in their fields and give their own take on what they believe are the most significant debates influencing research, drawing original conclusions.

Cambridge Elements ☰

Decision Theory and Philosophy

Elements in the Series

A full series listing is available at: www.cambridge.org/EDTP

Printed in the United States
by Baker & Taylor Publisher Services